George H. Puntenney

History of the Thirty-seventh regiment of Indiana infantry volunteers;

Its organization, campaigns, and battles--Sept. '61-Oct. '64

George H. Puntenney

History of the Thirty-seventh regiment of Indiana infantry volunteers;
Its organization, campaigns, and battles--Sept. '61-Oct. '64

ISBN/EAN: 9783337810658

Printed in Europe, USA, Canada, Australia, Japan

Cover: Foto ©ninafisch / pixelio.de

More available books at **www.hansebooks.com**

HISTORY

OF THE

Thirty=Seventh Regiment

OF

Indiana Infantry Volunteers

ITS ORGANIZATION, CAMPAIGNS, AND
BATTLES--SEPT., '61--OCT., '64.

Written by
SERGEANT GEORGE H. PUNTENNEY
At the request of his Comrades

RUSHVILLE, IND.:
Jacksonian Book and Job Department
1896

CONTENTS

	PAGE
PREFACE	6

CHAPTER I—Organization—Regimental and Company Officers—Marching Orders Received—Going to the River Through Lawrenceburg—Ride to Louisville 9

CHAPTER II—From Salt River to Elizabethtown—Thence to Bacon Creek—Much Sickness—The Colonel Arrested—Chaplain Lozier Arrested. ... 13

CHAPTER III—Marching to Bowling Green—Thence to Nashville................. 17

CHAPTER IV—Advance on Huntsville—Loyal Shelbyvillians—Huntsville Captured — The Sacking of Athens. 19

CHAPTER V—Marching Back to Fayettesville—Thence to Chattanooga—Captain W. D. Ward Captured. 28

CHAPTER VI—Battle of Stone River..... 33

CHAPTER VII—Guarding Murfreesboro — A Raid—Sunstroke—Hanging Two Men..... 38

CHAPTER VIII — Tullahoma Campaign — Gambling Mania—Colonel Hull Detailed—Brigade Stampeded by a Cow 44

CHAPTER IX—Chickamauga Campaign—Crossing the Tennessee River—Sand Mountain and Lookout Mountain — Skirmishing at Pigeon Mountain—Battle of Chickamauga........... 47

	PAGE
CHAPTER X—Siege of Chattanooga—Starving—Eating Cow Tails and Acorns.	62
CHAPTER XI—Atlanta Campaign—Buzzard Roost—Rocky Face—Battle of Resaca	81
CHAPTER XII—Army Moves Forward to Calhoun—Battle of Pumpkinvine Creek.	87
CHAPTER XIII—The Battle of Atlanta	110
CHAPTER XIV—The Siege of Atlanta	118
CHAPTER XV—Flank Movement—Fall of Atlanta and Jonesboro	125
CHAPTER XVI—An Incident	138
REGIMENTAL ROSTER	140
MARCH TO THE SEA	181

PREFACE

COMRADES of the Thirty-seventh Indiana Regiment, and all friends of that Regiment into whose hands this little volume may fall, permit me to assure you that I know full well that this little work which I dignify with the name "history" does not do you or that grand old Regiment even partial justice.

A complete history of all that you did, dared, endured and sacrificed in crushing the rebellion, and preserving for posterity the Government, purchased with the blood of Revolutionary fathers, will never be written. No man or number of men now living can do that.

I am also confident that many of my comrades could have written a better history than this, but that duty was not imposed upon them.

No doubt this history should contain many things which it does not; but I trust that it contains nothing that it should not. I have tried to write a history of the Thirty-seventh Regiment, and to exclude from it every word that might be offensive to any comrade.

The effort throughout has been to state, without ornamentation or exaggeration, as many plain and important facts as possible without partiality to any Company or person. If the history records more of the deeds of Company K than of other Companies, it is because the writer belonged to that Company, and not because he did not want to be fair with other Companies. Each enlisted man in the Regiment remembers more about his own Company than about other Companies.

I am greatly indebted to Comrades Colonel W. D. Ward; Leroy Roberts, of Company F; and T. B. Peery and John Wolverton, of Company E, and others, for many valuable facts and dates furnished me.

GEORGE H. PUNTENNEY.

W. C. PATTON, Co. K,
Greensburg, Ind.

Monumemt of the Thirty-seventh Indiana Regiment, erected in 1895, on the Chickamauga Battlefield, at the position taken by the Regiment on Saturday evening, September 19, 1863.

CHAPTER ONE

Organization—Regimental and Company Officers—Marching Orders Received—Going to the River Through Lawrenceburg—Ride to Louisville.

The war for the preservation of the Union had progressed only about four months when the Thirty-seventh Regiment of Indiana volunteers went into camp at Lawrenceburg. Some few companies went into camp about the 1st of August, 1861, and by the 18th of that month the Regiment contained nearly its full quota of strong young men. They were patriots who were determined to preserve the Union and crush that most wicked rebellion against their good government no matter what it should cost in blood and treasure. It was really inspiring to be associated with such strong, young and brave patriots. A few months after the organization of the Regiment, General Buell, after reviewing it, said it was as fine looking Regiment as he ever saw.

The Regiment was organized with George W. Hazzard, Colonel; Carter Gazlay, Lieutenant-Colonel; James S. Hull, Major; Livingston Howland, Adjutant; Francis Riddle, Quartermaster; John H. Lozier, Chaplain; William Anderson, Surgeon; John R. Goodwin, Assistant Surgeon. The commissioned Company officers were: Co. A, William D Ward, Captain; William Hyatt, First Lieutenant; Washington Stockwell, Second Lieutenant. Co. B, Thomas V. Kimble, Captain; Robert M. Goodwin, First Lieutenant; William H. Wilkinson, Second Lieutenant. Co. C, Thomas W. Pate, Captain; James T. Matteson, First Lieutenant; Robert C. Pate, Second Lieutenant. Co. D, Hezekiah Shook, Captain; Jesse B. Holman, First Lieutenant; James M. Hartley, Second Lieutenant. Co. E, Mahlon C. Connet, Captain; Frank Hughes, First Lieutenant; Andrew J. Hungate, Second Lieutenant. Co. F, Wesley G. Markland, Captain; John B. Hodges, First Lieutenant; Joseph P. Stoops, Second Lieutenant. Co. G, John McCoy, Captain; Archibald F. Allen, First Lieutenant; Daniel S. Shafer, Second Lieutenant. Co. H, William H. Tyner, Captain; Quartus C. Moore, First Lieutenant; George W. Pye, Second Lieutenant. Co. I, William N. Doughty, Captain; John Breaky, First Lieutenant; Isaac Abernathy, Second Lieutenant. Co. K, John McKee, Captain; Henry Lord, First Lieutenant; John B. Reeve, Second Lieutenant.

The Colonel was a regular army officer—a real soldier—a rigid disciplinarian, and just the man to teach officers and enlisted men how to conduct themselves in camp, on picket, on the march, on the skirmish line and on the field of battle. No doubt the Regiment owed much to this careful training for the brilliant record it afterwards made in many hard fought battles—a record on which there is not a single stain.

After drilling a month at Lawrenceburg, the Regiment, on the 18th day of September, 1861, was mustered into the United States service by taking the oath required. To be a real soldier, to be bound by a solemn oath to obey your superior officer, even if so doing led to death in a strange land, caused strange feelings to agitate the breasts of the young and honest farmers, merchants, and mechanics, of which the Regiment was largely composed But, for the love of their country, they cheerfully accepted the solemn obligation.

On the 19th of October, at dress parade, the following general order was read to the Regiment:

"HEADQUARTERS 37TH IND. VOL.,
Camp Dearborn, Oct. 19, 1861.
ORDER NO. 9.

The Colonel commanding congratulates the Regiment that they are ordered to take the field. Our first move will be to Louisville, Ky., and will be made tomorrow night. * * * By order of

L. HOWLAND, Adjutant.   COL. G. W. HAZZARD,

The next day knapsacks were packed, nearly every man having twice as much in his knapsack as he could carry, and not half as much as he thought he would need in order to be comfortable during the approaching winter. In the evening the Regiment formed and marched through Lawrenceburg to the river. Each man had a pack on his back as large as was carried years ago by traveling dry goods peddlers. Many good old ladies, with tears running down their motherly faces as the boys passed, audibly prayed that every one might be spared to return to parents and friends. The Regiment and teams were placed on a steamboat and two large barges that lay at the wharf, and steamed on down to Louisville. The night was extremely cold and the men suffered greatly. The boat arrived at Louisville before day, lay there most of the next day and then ran down to the mouth of Salt River.

CHAPTER TWO

From Salt River to Elizabethtown Thence to Bacon Creek—Much Sickness Drilling The Colonel Arrested—Chaplain Lozier Arrested.

At Salt River the Regiment drilled and worked on Muldraugh's Hill a few weeks, and then moved on to Elizabethtown, Ky. From there it went to Bacon Creek, Ky. The men had been greatly exposed during all the time since they left Lawrenceburg. They were not allowed to gather straw for beds, and had to sleep on the ground in their tents through November and December, and many of them died at Bacon Creek during the months of December and January. At Bacon Creek twelve men died in one night in the hospital tent, and their bodies were laid out on a rail pile near by. Both Col. Hazzard and Dr. Anderson were to blame for some of the exposure of the men. Consequently, both the Colonel and the Doctor were heartily disliked by most of the enlisted men. The Colonel would not permit any of his men to eat anything but government rations. It was a serious offense to buy cake, pie, fowl or fish from a citizen. If the Colonel found any man coming into camp with provision he would make him throw it away.

One day a Co. H man, named Daily, who could imitate to perfection the noise of any barn-yard fowl, came past the Colonel's tent with his oil blanket full of leaves for his bed. As he passed the tent, a noise in the blanket sounded very much like a hen was confined there. The Colonel rushed out, and with much profanity assured the man that he had caught him disobeying orders and ordered him to let that hen go.

Daily dropped the leaves, but no hen ran out, and the Colonel "caught on" and sneaked back into his tent.

December came in cold and cheerless, and Jacob S. McCullough, Co. K's poet, sympathizing with the gloomy surroundings and discouraging prospect, repeated the poet's melancholy words, "The cold, chilly winds of December," which were often repeated by many in the Regiment for a few weeks.

Lieut. W. H. Baughman, Co. G.
Richmond, Ind.

The colder it got the more dissatisfied the men became, and the more vigorous was the Colonel's discipline. Consequently, the men were more than delighted one day when Col. Turchin, commanding the brigade, gave a command which they did not understand, and Hazzard rushed furiously at him, saying: "There is no such command in the book."

Then Col. Turchin coolly said: "Col. Hazzard, you must not address your superior officer in that way; give me your sword; consider yourself under arrest and go to your quarters." He rode off and the men in the Regiment could scarcely keep from cheering. Turchin was ever afterwards a great favorite with the Thirty-Seventh Regiment.

While in camp at Bacon Creek, Chaplain John H. Lozier wrote an article, which was published in the

Cincinnati Commercial, criticising the conduct of the Colonel and Surgeon. For this, the Colonel placed the Chaplain under arrest; placed charges against him, and had him fined. The boys made up the fine for their Chaplain, and thus showed that they believed in him.

Shortly after this Dr. Blackburn, of Cincinnati, the medical director of the division to which the 37th belonged, came into camp, and riding up to Dr. Anderson's quarters, called him out and said: "Doctor, don't you know better than to put your sick men in such a hovel as they are in?" Dr. Blackburn, continuing, said: "It is outrageous; worse than the Black Hole of Calcutta." Then Col. Hazzard came out and said he did not allow any one to interfere with his Regiment. Dr Blackburn said: "I will come in whenever I please." Hazzard said: "Leave my camp." "I will when I get ready," Dr. Blackburn said. The Colonel turned to Grossman, of Co. A, and said: "Bring me a file of guards." The file of guards was brought, and when Dr. Blackburn got ready to go, he turned to Col. Hazzard and said in bitterest sarcasm: "Colonel, have you that escort ready?"

David S. Stewart, Co. K. Richland, Ind.

The Colonel ordered the Corporal to take the Doctor out of camp, which he did. In about an hour, Gen. Mitchell, our division commander, rode into camp and had a brief talk with Col. Hazzard in his tent, and left. Soon afterwards Col. Turchin and several of his staff rode into camp, and calling Col. Hazzard out of his tent, placed him under arrest in the presence and hearing of a large number of officers and private soldiers. This was loudly cheered by many of the soldiers. Major Hull said the cheering "was done by a d—d set of low-flung privates."

After the removal of Hazzard, the health of the Regiment improved rapidly and discontentment disappeared.

CHAPTER THREE

The March to Bowling Green—Thence to Nashville.

On the 12th of Feb., 1862, the Regiment was ordered to move with three days' rations to attack the Confederates at Bowling Green, Ky. The Regiment started early next morning and marched to Cave City that day, where it bivouacked for the night.

The first night out was warm the fore part of the night, and the men being tired, slept soundly. The snow commenced falling about midnight and covered, but did not awake the tired hosts. The bugle awoke them in the morning, and as they shook the snow from their garments, each boasted of his good night's rest, and prepared for the day's march. The rebels having learned of our advance, burned the bridge that spanned Barron River, opposite the city, and our brigade marched a few miles down the river and found an old boat in which it crossed the stream with great difficulty by working all night, going into the city at daylight. Nearly all the houses were vacated, and, of course, the boys did not sleep out of doors at night nor suffer for provision. Meat and flour and meal and cooking utensils were there in abundance and the army feasted.

Before starting down the river a battery was planted and fired at a train in the city loaded with military stores and just ready to leave. A ball struck the engine and disabled it. This caused the rebels to burn the train and depot, filled with trunks and military stores. They had a strong skirmish line on their side of the river, which caused the Thirty-Seventh to hear the first whistle of rebel bullets. The exposure and marching had been too great for Sergeant John F. Lingenfelter, of Co. K, who took pneumonia and died Feb. 23, 1862. He was a noble and brave patriot, loved by all his comrades. As one of the Regiments marched into town preceded by its band, a citizen asked Capt. Ward: "What are you'uns playing we'uns tune for?" The Captain replied: "It is our tune; we are going down into Dixie, and intend to stay there."

From Bowling Green the Regiment marched on to Nashville, Tenn. The rebels had cut down the fine suspension bridge that spanned the Cumberland River, which was high, and was crossed with great difficulty. But the weather was getting warm and delightful, and the beautiful southland, and Nashville—the home of Jackson and James K. Polk—seemed to inspire the men of the Thirty-Seventh with cheer and hope.

While in camp near Nashville, three men, W. D. Elrod, H. S. Lane and James Harper, were captured while outside of the lines by a force of cavalry. A battalion of Federal cavalry pursued, and while a lively skirmish was going on the three prisoners escaped, Lane having received a severe wound in the neck.

About the 5th of March, 1862, Col. Hazzard received orders from the War Department to report for duty to his command in the Regular Army. Gen. Buell released him from arrest that he might obey the order, but instead of doing it he assumed command of the Regiment. Col. Ward, then Captain, being officer of the day, was ordered to tell our old Colonel to give up the command, which he did, and Col. Hazzard called for his horse, rode away and was never seen again by any one of the Regiment. He was Captain of a battery in the Eastern Army, to which he returned and was killed, it is said, in the seven days' battle before Richmond.

CHAPTER FOUR

Advance on Huntsville, Ala.—Going Through the Enemy's Country—Loyal Shelbyvillians—Huntsville Captured—Sacking of Athens.

The brigade to which the Thirty-Seventh Ind. belonged at this time was composed of the following Regiments: The Nineteenth Ills.; The Twenty-Fourth Ills.; the Eighteenth Ohio and the Thirty-Seventh Ind.

About the last of March, 1862, the division to which this brigade was attached, commanded by Gen. O. M. Mitchell, the author of "Mitchell's Geography," which most of his soldiers had studied, was taken from Gen. Buell's army and sent south to Huntsville, Ala.

We marched south by easy stages, meeting an almost universal rebel sentiment until we reached Shelbyville, Tenn., where the citizens met us with our flag and welcomed us with great delight. The Union sentiment was so strong there that the rebels called it New Boston.

The friendship of these people made us feel like we were near home. They were like Northern people, and they dearly loved the old flag and the Union.

From Shelbyville we went to Fayetteville, Tenn., and remained there a few days. April 5th, 1862, we started for Huntsville, Ala. It rained incessantly all day, and so we marched all day through mud and swollen streams. We doubt if there was anything on any one that day was dry but his powder. We were then in the heart of the enemy's country, with no friends but the poor negroes, and we had to be prepared all the time for battle.

About dusk the evening before we got to Huntsville we came to a stream, across which there was no bridge, and in which the water was fully four feet deep. Gen. Mitchell was in a hurry, and his army must cross, no matter how deep and cold the water was. The men good naturedly took off their coats, shoes, stockings and pants (their shirts were not much longer than their vests, and there was no need to remove them), and holding up their guns, cartridge boxes, haversacks and clothing, plunged into the water with a whoop and came out on the other side. There they built fires, warmed and put on their clothing, ate a little supper and pushed forward, marching all night, and arrived at Huntsville at daylight the next morning, taking the citizens by surprise. The first intimation they had of our presence was the heavy tramp of the soldiers on the streets. It is said that one old lady, hearing the noise, looked out of her window and exclaimed: "Oh, Lord! what big men; no wonder we'uns can't fight 'um."

The citizens received the soldiers civilly but coldly, while the colored people could not conceal their delight at seeing us, and did not seem to try to do so. One old colored woman came rushing along, and with tears running down her cheeks, shouted: "Glory to God! Glory to God! I'se been praying for dis dose many years." The citizens were not friendly, but quite submissive. To swoop down on a large city, take charge of it and require the citizens to act as you dictate to them, gives one a good idea of the prerogatives of war.

We captured at Huntsville a large number of prisoners, nineteen locomotives and much rolling stock. The rebels disabled most of the captured engines, but there were plenty of machinists in our division, and in a short time they had these engines in good order again. Our brigade was soon put on a train of cars—platform and stock cars—and hurried to the railroad bridge that crossed the Tennessee River at Decatur, Ala. We were there in time to prevent the burning of it, and the next day we went west to Tuscumbia. That town is surrounded by a fine country and large plantations. Some of the negro quarters of a single plantation contained ten or fifteen little houses or homes for the slaves. At Huntsville we saw the first whipping post to which negroes were tied while being whipped.

At Tuscumbia we saw the first trained blood hounds. They were kept in a little pen, and looked as if they would, as a little darkey said, "Eat a niggah up in a minute, shore." We made several raids on different parts of the country around Tuscumbia for several days, but nothing of importance occurred till one day a large force of the enemy moved onto us and we were ordered to fall back to Decatur. In the meantime a barrel of whisky was captured, and the Colonel, Gazley, not being a strict temperance man, knocked in the barrel's head and let the boys fill their canteens with the stuff. Some of the boys, not many of them, got drunk, and it was believed that Capt. W. D. Ward, afterwards Colonel, was the maddest man in either army. After crossing a stream called Big Nance, some of the men were quite drunk and had to be cared for. Fortunately there were not many in that condition. Most men in the Regiment considered getting drunk almost as disgraceful as playing the coward in front of the enemy.

As we were the first Union soldiers those Southerners had seen, we had a good opportunity to learn something of the feeling of Southern people for Northern soldiers. And it is safe to say that most Southern people actually hated the Northern soldiers, and Northern people. The best citizens of the South would do all in their power to deceive our soldiers.

Women turned up their pretty noses at our men when they met them. One woman in Huntsville deliberately spit on a soldier one day, and he simply knocked her down. No more soldiers were spit on. But those ladies soon got over their prejudices, and soon afterwards the best-looking ladies of Huntsville were seen walking the streets escorted by some blue-coated officer or soldier, and in a number of instances those Southern ladies married those Northern soldiers: all of which goes to show that those ladies were not only good looking, but smart, and knew a good thing when they saw it.

Wm. Rowland, Co. F, North Indianapolis, Ind. Wounded at Battle Stone River, Dec. 31, 1862. Discharged March 31, 1863.

While at Huntsville our boys captured the rebel mails two or three times, and reading those captured letters was pasttime with some of us. Those letters showed just what the people down there were. While many of the writers of the letters were evidently illiterate and coarse, many of them were scholarly and refined. Some of the letters from parents to sons, and from sons to parents, showed that their writers were intelligent christians, unfortunately engaged in a bad cause. As a sort of war measure the people at Huntsville had issued a large number of pasteboard cards on which were printed: "Good for 10 cents;" sometimes for a larger amount, and when any one got $5 worth of such cards with some merchant's name on them, they were redeemed with a Confederate $5 bill. The Nineteenth Ills. boys got a printing press and some pasteboard, and expanded the circulation till no man's name on a card was worth a penny. While at Huntsville the 37th Regiment and the brigade received orders to go to the relief of the 18th Ohio, which had been attacked at Athens by a large force of rebels. Our Regiment, commanded by Major W. D. Ward, who had been recently promoted from Captain, and the rest of the brigade, all under command of Col. Turchin, took the cars and went to the nearest point to Athens. From there we marched all night toward that town, and at daylight met the 18th Ohio slowly falling back before a superior force of the enemy.

The brigade formed for action, and it was not long before the rebels were making a much more rapid retreat than the 18th Ohio had been making. They were driven several miles beyond Athens, when we returned to the town. Col. Turchin, who commanded the brigade, ordered Major Ward, of the 37th Ind., and Col. Mihilotski, of the 24th Ills., to take their commands to a position some distance from the town, which they did. The 19th Ills. and the 18th Ohio were left in the town, and the men of those Regiments say that Col. Turchin rode among them and remarked to

S. R. Patton, Co. K. Richland, Ind.

the boys: "I see nothing for two hours." Whether he said that or not is not certainly known, but it is certain that at the expiration of the two hours there was not much of value to be seen in Athens. Not during all the remainder of the war was such wanton destruction of property seen by those men.

Men who had been sleeping in the mud, laid fine broadcloth on the ground that night and slept on it. Everything of value was carried out of dry goods stores, jewelry stores and drug stores. Will Scott, of Co. K. bought a fine gold watch of one of the 19th Ills. men for a few dollars of Confederate scrip, which he got at Huntsville. The sidewalks of the town were almost covered with dry goods. A 19th Ills. man (not Gov. Chase, who belonged to the 19th), who evidently would not have pleaded not guilty to the charge of assisting in the sacking of Athens, is described as follows by a 37th Ind. soldier:

The "sucker" had evidently been at a drug store. He was tall and slender, and had dressed himself in a fine pair of cloth pants, a vest and boots, and a striped pigeon-tailed coat far too big for him at the shoulders, but too short, the tails of the coat only coming to his waist. He also wore a silk stove pipe hat, around which he had wrapped one end of a richly-colored ribbon, three inches in width, the rest of the bolt of ribbon streaming out behind him as he swaggered and staggered up the street singing "The girl I left behind me." He had started out "to make treason odious, and to let the proud rebels of Athens know that while the soldiers of the Union were always obedient to orders and deferential to ladies, they could resent insults when so minded." It is doubtful if any Northern soldier during the war, did more to offend and disgust Southern ladies than did this 19th Ills. soldier; and that was just

what he wanted to do. The sacking of Athens has often been condemned even by men in the North, but whether it was right or wrong, it had a good effect on the rebels, and was about what those Athenian rebels deserved. For the first year or two our armies dealt entirely too leniently with them.

The 18th Ohio had been left there to guard the town, protect rebel property, which it most faithfully did. While doing this they were insulted in almost every conceivable way, even fired upon by citizens from houses that soldiers were guarding. News was sent to a large rebel force to come and kill and capture their protectors. After Athens was looted, no other Southern town mistreated any of the Regiments of Turchin's Brigade. Southerners simply called them "Turchin's thieves."

The Nineteenth Illinois Regiment did not do all the plundering that was done at Athens, for many men of the Thirty-seventh Indiana and Twenty-fourth Illinois, got into the town and took a hand in the work. Afterwards, when the General commanding called the officers of these Regiments to account for the conduct of their commands, Col. Gazley convinced him that the only part that the Thirty-seventh Regiment took in the business was the taking by a few men of a little molasses out of a store that was broken into. Thus the 37th escaped with a slight reprimand, while the 24th Ills., and especially the 19th Ills., received pretty severe punishment. Ever afterwards when the 24th Ills. would meet the 37th, they would say in their soft German (it was a German Regiment), to the 37th: "Molasses."

While at Athens, most of the Brigade camped in the amphitheater of the race track for a few days, and the sports had great fun running the cavalry horses, which a general order promptly stopped. While at Athens the 37th started one morning to meet a provision train and escort it into camp. The distance from Athens was more than twenty miles.

We arrived at our destination that evening and ate supper just as the sun was sinking out of sight. Just then a messenger arrived on a horse fleaked with foam, with orders for the Regiment to march back with all haste to Athens, as an attack was expected the next morning. Back the tired men started, and after marching all night, got back to camp the next morning at sun up, having marched in twenty-four hours not much less than fifty miles. The whole Brigade was formed in line of battle waiting for Gen. Forest, who had wisely abandoned his contemplated attack. Perhaps no Regiment in either army made a longer march in twenty-four hours during the war than that. Of course a goodly number of men fell out of the ranks before reaching Athens; some of them marched while sleeping, and becoming weary, unconsciously stepped aside and laid down to sleep.

About this time forty-nine men of Co. E. of the 37th, were sent a few miles from the main camp to guard a railroad bridge, or rather a high trestle, at a place now called, I understand, Elkins—Lieut. Frank Hughes in command. After remaining there a few days, Capt. Connett, having joined his command, the Company was attacked by the 15th Kentucky Cavalry and 120 Texas Rangers, numbering in all 720 men, commanded by Col. Woodward, of Kentucky. After fighting fiercely half an hour they surrendered. The loss of the enemy had been so heavy that some of them, from excessive anger, perhaps, did not cease firing until they shot after the surrender and severely wounded B. C. Whitlow, causing him to lose an eye. Five men of Company E, James Jordon, John T. Morgan, J. R. Conner, A. O. Scull and

Robert F. Heaton, were killed, and Capt. Connett, John F. Wolverton, Marion Garrett, James Hanger, James Tillison and perhaps others were wounded. Captain Connett was wounded seven times before he surrendered. Indeed, he did not surrender; he was simply overpowered. The rebels lost forty in killed and wounded, losing a man for every man they killed or wounded or captured. Thus it will be seen that the fight was very fierce, and creditable to Co. E, the Thirty-seventh Regiment, and all Indiana soldiers.

The captured men were taken to Tuscaloosa, thence to Montgomery, and thence to Macon, Ga., where they remained prisoners five months before they were exchanged, and returned to their Regiment All came back more determined than before to crush treason and rebellion, and restore the Union. It is seldom that greater bravery is displayed than was displayed by the men of that company on that occasion.

CHAPTER FIVE

Marching Back to Fayetteville and Thence to Chattanooga—Capt. W. D. Ward Captured.

Sometime in May the Regiment returned to Fayetteville, Tenn. A number of Regiments besides those of our Brigade were collected there for a raid on Chattanooga, Tenn. The 37th was commanded by Col. Gazley and Col. Ward. We marched across the mountains to the Sequatchie Valley, and from thence across the Cumberland Mountains to the Tennessee river, and in sight of Chattanooga.

A battery was placed on a spur of the mountain and opened fire on the city, and a body of Infantry formed on the bank of the river and fired across it at the troops on the other side. The next day we were ordered back to Stevenson, Ala., to which place we went, and the 37th was distributed along the railroad to guard bridges across Crow Creek, with headquarters at Stevenson. Occasionally detachments were sent to patrol and guard the banks of the Tennessee river.

I believe it was on the 3rd day of July, 1862, while Col. Ward was in command of one of these detachments, guarding the bank of the Tennessee river, that he was captured. He had learned that the Confederates had a large amount of corn and some horses on an island just below him, and he determined to capture them if possible. No boats being on the north side of the river, W. D. Elrod and another soldier swam the river after dark and brought over an old dug-out. Col. Ward and Elrod, with nothing on but pants and shirt, crossed the river. The Colonel crawled cautiously up the bank. In attempting to return his boat struck an obstacle near the bank, and the noise aroused the guards, who captured him. He said his captors treated him kindly, gave him an old straw hat and a pair of shoes. The guard who captured him and an officer took him to Gen. Heath, at Chattanooga. While on the way there an old lady came running to see him, and after looking at him a few moments, said: "You can't fool me. He's no Yankee." Turning to the officer, who wore a blue coat, she said: "You are the Yankee," and would consent to nothing else. He was placed in the guard house with some rebel soldiers. The next day his men on the north side of the river sent over to him his uniform under a flag of truce, after which the Colonel said he was given the liberty of the camp on his parol. He was taken from there to Knoxville, to Gen. Kirby Smith. The Colonel said he got permission while at Knoxville to purchase a long linen coat and cap with which he concealed his identity, and thus escaped criticisms and many insults from citizens and soldiers.

From there he was taken to Madison, Ga., and his guards were ordered to protect him from all insults and injuries, which they did. This special favor, his captors informed him, was granted because of his kindness to citizens and prisoners at Huntsville while he was in command at that place of which they had heard. Several persons who had been the recipients of his kindness called on him and thanked him, and one old gentleman gave him a bottle of wine, which the Colonel accepted, but being a strict temperance man, turned over to Confederates to drink. He remained in that prison till October, and was taken to Richmond, where he was exchanged. After spending some time with his family and friends, he returned to his command at Nashville, Tenn., about the middle of December.

As before stated, the Thirty-seventh Regiment was scattered along the river and railroads, and it would be impossible to give a history of its acts for some weeks without giving a history of each company. They had during that time many strange adventures and funny experiences. Thus, one night when Co. K was camped in a cave of the mountain at Stevenson, guarding a large spring of water and the water tank, after all but the one sentinel was wrapped in sleep, he called for the "Corporal of the guard" so loud as to awake every one in the camp. The mountain on every side but the front made it very dark.

Right close to the rear of the camp, at the foot of the mountain, some beast was heard making a great noise, rather more like a vicious snort than a growl, but really frightful. Capt. McKee called on every man to come forth armed to defend the camp.

W. N. Stewart, Quartermaster Sergeant, Richland, Ind.

The most incredulous could not doubt that a large, ravenous and fearless beast had come down the mountain in search of prey. The thought of an Indiana soldier being killed by a wild beast from the Cumberland Mountains caused feelings of both fear and shame to agitate our breasts. To abandon the camp was not to be thought of for a moment. So the Captain's call was responded to with alacrity. Though it was so dark that no one could see anything, yet every man grabbed his gun, and fixing his bayonet, began with thumping heart to move cautiously toward the beast that was snorting and growling but a few steps away. At last one man, feeling sure that he was in reach of the animal, and seeing its outline through the darkness, lunged at it with his bayonet, and if ever a hog squealed and ran, that one did. The old hog had something the matter with its nose that caused it to make an ugly, snarling noise.

So far as can be learned the boys of the other companies of the Regiment put in the time guarding the river, railroad bridges, saluting officers and passing trains, playing cards, catching the ague and shaking til about the 1st of September, when the Regiment was collected at Cowan, and with the whole army marched back to Nashville, Tenn. But before doing so, Cowan was badly, and, I thought, harshly treated. Many houses were set on fire, and much property destroyed, though I believe the commanding officers did what they could to prevent it.

John Johnson, Co. H.

The army was under strict discipline while at Nashville, and the guards' duty very heavy. For several weeks in October and November every able-bodied soldier was required to get up at 4 o'clock in the morning and march out some distance from the city, and stand in the cold or rain till after daylight. Foraging and guard duty formed the daily and nightly routine of soldier life at Nashville; and the genuine soldier dislikes guard duty about as much as he likes foraging Not much of eatables for man or beast were left on the fine farms around Nashville when the army left for Murfreesboro. Comrade John Morton, of Co. C, gives the following humorous description of a foraging expedition in which he was engaged. He says:

"While the 37th was quartered in the railroad depot at Nashville during the fall of '62, doing garrison duty while Gen. Bragg made his famous raid into Kentucky, it was our custom to frequently make trips out into the country, sometimes by way of the "Grany White" pike; but on this occasion we went out on the "Hardie" road. Our duties were to procure forage for both man and beast. It was my luck (you may call it good fortune—I don't) to capture a Billy goat; also some cornmeal, and after returning to camp we managed to get one of those "Dutch ovens" with its heavy lid, in order to properly bake our cornmeal pone. We accordingly prepared the batch, and to make it as rich as possible mixed in large quantities of the fat of the goat after baking, being very hungry. Oh, what a feast! You all know that one of the peculiarities of those Dutch ovens is to preserve all of the "aroma" of its contents. Suffice it to say I have not been subject to any contagious diseases since that memorable evening in the fall of 1862."

John Morton, Co. C.
Pueblo, Col.

CHAPTER SIX

The Battle of Stone River on the 31st—Fighting Begins—Men Piled Knapsacks.

On the 26th of December, 1862, the Regiment and about all the army received orders to march on to Murfreesboro. That was understood by all to mean a battle, for it was well known that a large force of the enemy was there. Everything went on smoothly until about dark of the 29th day of December, when we found ourselves in close proximity to the enemy. A strange and indescribably solemn feeling always pervades an army when it knows that it is in the immediate neighborhood of a strong and brave foe. Without knowing it, men converse in a lower tone of voice, and words and actions which on ordinary occasions would not be noticed, become exceedingly funny and ridiculous. The next day, Dec. 30th, was spent in forming the battle lines and skirmishing with the enemy, which seemed rather to invite than evade the attack.

We lay that night in our cold, cheerless bivouac, and before daylight on the morning of the 31st, were up and in line of battle waiting for the enemy. Not long did we wait. It was scarcely clear daylight when on our right the awful roar of cannon, and the sharp rattle of thousands of rifles told us plainly that the battle had begun, and in a very short time the great crowd of demoralized soldiers running to the rear, announced that disaster had occurred on that part of our line.

Then the men were ordered to pile their knapsacks that they might be the better prepared for the fray, which was done. Then it was ordered into a cedar thicket to check, and hold in check the advancing enemy.

The Regiment had scarcely got into position when the Confederates, flushed with their success on our right, assailed the Thirty-seventh with all the pride and determination of the Southern soldiers. The conflict was fierce, close and bloody. It seemed for a time that the enemy would sweep our brave men from the field, but the brave fellows stood and poured volley after volley into their lines, and taught them to approach more cautiously that part of the army of the Union.

Failing to drive our brave boys from their position, the enemy—a rebel brigade on our left, marched out of an open woods, and fronting on our left flank prepared to charge us. To meet this, the left company of the Thirty-seventh changed front to face the enemy, and the Seventy-fourth Ohio, commanded by Col. Granville Moody, formed on the left of this company, and gave the enemy such a reception as they had not expected, and such a one as made them move cautiously in the future. Col. Moody was an old Methodist preacher, and as they began the advance on the enemy, he, swinging his sword high over his head, shouted at the top of his voice: "Come on, christian brethern," and right gallantly did his men follow him.

Just about this time the rebel column in front of the Thirty-seventh renewed their attack most fiercely, and the battle also raged furiously on the left company and on the Seventy-fourth Ohio. Our brave men were falling fast, but the survivors would not yield a single inch. The rebel brigade that moved on our left had passed on till it came to the front of the Twenty-first Ohio, which was armed with Colt's revolving rifles, and lay concealed in a thicket. When that Regiment opened on them they laid down, but not being able to endure the merciless fire, broke and ran in confusion, leaving many of their number on the field. While the fighting at this point was at the fiercest—when shot and shell and minnie balls were flying thickest, an Irishman of the Seventy-fourth Ohio said to Col. Moody: "Colonel, you have been fighting the devil for twenty years, and don't you think hell has broke loose now?"

The rebel line in our front was driven back two or three different times, and rallied and came again. Then the Thirty-seventh was ordered back for some reason, passing over ground that had been fought over by troops in its rear, unknown to the Regiment. As the Regiment was going back Col. Hull was wounded and Lieutenant-Colonel Ward took command, and led the Regiment back and supplied it with ammunition, and took position with the reserve.

Perhaps the Thirty-seventh never did harder fighting than it did at that time and place. Three times the rebels charged it, and three times were repulsed. Most men of the Thirty-seventh fired sixty rounds while there. The horses of Col. Hull, Lieutenant-Colonel Ward and Major Kimble were all killed or disabled there. As the rebels charged our line and received our fire, men could be seen stumbling and falling dead or wounded. The loss of the Thirty-seventh at that point was very heavy. No Regiment in that great and good army behaved better than the Thirty-seventh did. Col. Ward says:

"This was the gloomiest time I ever remember to have experienced. We had had a very bloody engagement; we knew quite a number had been killed and many more had been wounded, but of the many not 'present' we could not tell who were killed or wounded. The right of the army had been broken; yes, routed, and not knowing how it happened, we did not know what to expect. The lines were reformed in the shape of an immense horse-shoe, but would not that part of the army which had been driven once, break again if assailed again? These reflections made the outlook gloomy, indeed."

The night passed with slight skirmishing, and the next day both armies seemed more cautious and the conflict was less deadly. But it was evident the next morning that the conflict would be fierce and perhaps decisive. A train arrived with rations, and the Thirty-seventh, which had little to eat for two days, the officers faring no better than the men, were supplied with flour. This was mixed in water into dough, and cooked on hot rocks as best it could be and eaten. Meat was roasted or eaten raw with a relish. While trying to satisfy the cravings of hunger the Regiment was ordered into line and to double quick over to the left to meet an expected charge. Arriving at that point the Regiment found about sixty cannon there and in position, behind which a short distance the Regiment took position.

In a few minutes the Confederates under Gen. Breckenridge fiercely assailed the Federal lines south of Stone River and drove them back to it. Here they were met by our division—Negley's, and some other troops, and after severe fighting were turned back, and driven by our forces until night closed the fighting. During the night a rain set in, and Stone River rose rapidly and that part of our army that was on the south side of the river, being liable to be cut off, by reason of high water, from the rest of the army, and thus left to contend with the whole rebeled army, was moved back to the north side of the river. That was a dark, dismal night, the men without fire or covering, lying on the ground while a cold rain poured down upon them. But like true soldiers, they bore it manfully, and when daylight came, cheerfully ate their coarse food and stood ready for whatever duty or trial the day might have in store for them.

Desultory fighting continued throughout the day, and towards evening it was evident that the enemy was massing troops at some point preparatory to making a night attack. There was some lively skirmishing that night and the rebels were driven at many points, but there was no general engagement. The Thirty-seventh Ind. camped that night just south of town in a clover field, and the rebel army slipped away under cover of the darkness. The battle had been fought and won and the Federal Army was victorious, but at a fearful sacrifice of life.

The loss of the Thirty-seventh was heavy. It went into the battle with 456 officers and men, 156 of whom were either killed or wounded. The loss of the Federal Army was 1,500 killed and something over 7,000 wounded. The Confederate loss was even greater. Rosecrans said his army numbered 43,000, Bragg's army was larger, but just what the number was is not known.

The Thirty-seventh Ind. and the other Regiments of the State and of other States, proved in that battle that the citizen soldiers of the peace-loving North were not inferior to the best soldiers the world ever produced. The Thirty-seventh was the first Regiment in Murfreesboro. Col. Hull, of the Thirty-seventh Ind., was severely wounded early in the engagement, and Lieutenant-Colonel Ward, who commanded the Regiment after the Colonel was disabled, had his horse shot from under him, got a bullet hole through his overcoat and had a minnie ball to graze his chin, but was not seriously hurt.

CHAPTER SEVEN

Guarding Murfreesboro—A Raid Sunstroke—Hanging Two Men.

Joseph Blair, Co. K, Rushville, Ind.

The 37th Regiment remained near town for some time, acting as provost guard. Provost duty—guarding houses and private property, policing camp, blacking old shoes, wearing white gloves at inspections is just what the hardy and honorable volunteer soldiers, especially Hoosier soldiers, abominates. But the Thirty-seventh did all these distasteful duties well, but was always glad when called to go on a scout or raid of some kind. One time while the Regiment was at Murfreesboro, it and a Michigan Regiment were ordered out on a scout some fifteen miles from that town. The Thirty-seventh took the advance going, and the Michigan Regiment was accorded that position as we returned. Nothing of any consequence came of the raid and after eating dinner, both Regiments started back to camp.

The Thirty-seventh took the advance on returning for a couple of miles, and stepped to one side of the road to give the Michigan Regiment a chance to move to the front. That Regiment had not seen much hard service; the men were fat and unused to hardships, and the day was fearfully hot. As the men of that Regiment moved through the Thirty-seventh to the front, one of its men was sunstruck, and fell down by the roadside and struggled as if he were dying. One of his comrades, a large, fleshy man, who was stripped to his shirt, and red as a lobster, coming up and seeing the sunstruck man lying and gasping, asked "What's the matter with that man?" On being told "Sunstroke," he said, wiping his brow with his sleeve: "I wish to G—d I could git one of them things."

While at Murfreesboro Chaplain Lozier was acting as Division Postmaster. There was no regularity in the coming or going of the mails, and consequently the inquiries as to when the mail would go out became frequent and annoying. To answer this inquiry once and for all, the Chaplain placed on a piece of pasteboard in large letters: "The Chaplain does not know when the mail will go," and hung it in front of his tent. Soon after, while he was out on business, a fun-loving, but not overly-pious soldier, wrote immediately under this, in the same kind of letters, "Neither does he care a damn." One can readily imagine the surprise of the Chaplain when he returned and saw the amendment the witty soldier had made to his notice. He could not swear, and did not feel like praying, and simply took the notice down and afterwards answered all questions by the living voice.

John Cowan, First Sergeant Co. H, Bath P. O., Franklin County, Indiana.

While at Murfreesboro, two men who had been convicted of murder at McMinville, Tenn., and were awaiting execution in jail, were released by Union soldiers who thought they had been put in there because they were Union men. When the fact was known, they were recaptured and put in jail at Murfreesboro, and after a time were hanged by the Thirty-seventh. How it became the duty of the military to hang these men I do not know, but the Thirty-seventh did it. On the 5th day of June, 1863, the Regiment took one of them, A. S. Selkirk, to the scaffold. He was placed on his coffin in an army wagon and taken into a woods, guarded by a large detachment of the Thirty-seventh Ind. There the gallows had been erected, and a rope swung from a beam above. The wagon was driven under this and stopped so that the hind end gate of the wagon, when let down horizontally, would be under the cross beam. Nearly every soldier in the army who was not on duty, had got a pass to go and see the man hanged. Such a sight is seldom ever seen and not less than 10,000 men were there.

Every tree near the gallows that could be climbed was almost covered with soldiers sitting on the limbs. Thousands surged around the wagon. The Thirty-seventh had to fix bayonets and drive them back. It then formed a "hollow square" and the poor mortal walked out on the end gate, was bound hand and foot, and after prayer by a Chaplain, was swung into eternity. A young lady, whose father this man had killed for money, stood close to the drop, and a smile played on her face as the man struggled in death. The other condemned man was hanged from the same gallows a few days afterwards,

CHAPTER EIGHT

Tullahoma Campaign—A Gambling Mania—Col. Hull Detailed—Brigade Stampeded by a Cow.

Bragg's army was holding a position on Duck River, and we were all glad when orders came to advance. On the 24th of June, 1863, we struck tents and started with our division (Negley's) and the rest of the army to hunt Bragg. He was not hard to find, and though there was some sharp fighting at Hoover's Gap, the Thirty-seventh was not engaged. We laid in a wheat field the next night, and the boys slept on wheat shocks for bedding.

On the 26th we camped at Beech Grove, and on the 27th Negley's division went on a reconnoissance several miles to a farm house, where we remained about an hour and returned. The next day the enemy was found just where we had been the day before. Our Regiment, with all of Thomas' corps, arrived at Manchester about midnight. From thence we went to Tullahoma, and on the night of the 28th or 29th, lay in an open field with a dense woods in front of us. In the morning we were called into line of battle, and formed near the edge of the woods.

The artillerymen were burnishing their guns; field officers were riding hurriedly from point to point, and the skirmishers in the dense forest were firing quite briskly and everything looked as if a battle were imminent. But there was no battle and we marched on. About July 1st the Thirty-seventh made a forced march of some miles to re-inforce the first Brigade of our division, which was sharply engaged. We double-quicked in the direction of the firing beneath a broiling sun, and many men were overcome with the heat. We saw a large number of dead and wounded, but did no fighting. It looked strange to see our boys hunting and eating huckleberries in the open woods where we were and where several poor, wounded soldiers lay and suffered.

We here became impressed with the fact that Bragg had evacuated Tullahoma and was trying to get his army across the Cumberland mountains. It was shortly after leaving Tullahoma that rations gave out and the boys, as Negley rode past, said in loud tones: "Hard tack," and he showed so much temper. We crossed the river on a dilapidated old bridge, and camped for a short time where our cavalry had had a sharp skirmish. Several Confederate dead were yet where they fell near a farm house.

Leroy Roberts, of Co. F, and a few others took in the sights at that place, and say they were sad, indeed. We reached Dechard, Tenn., the 3d day of July, and were ordered into camp. No one can tell just how tired the men were. They had marched and counter-marched through rain and mud for nearly two weeks, and slept like hogs in mud and water and that order was greatly enjoyed and cheerfully obeyed. On the morning of the Fourth of July, 1863, as the army was quietly resting, the deep boom of cannon was heard in the distance, and all expected to be called immediately to fall in and move to the scene of conflict, when an officer rode into camp and said that Vicksburg had fallen into the hands of the Union army, and that the Eastern army had gained a glorious victory at Gettysburg. No one enjoyed victories and news of victories more than the soldier boys, and the day was one of hilarity. Victories brightened the prospect, sometimes exceedingly dim, of returning to home and friends and peace, all in a loved and united country.

While at Dechard the mail arrived and brought news of home and of the Morgan raid through Indiana. At this place the Regiment was put under strict army regulations—company and regimental drill, dress parade, policing grounds, guard duty, brightening guns, etc. And, strange as it may seem, here under this strict discipline the soldiers developed such a passion for gambling that the officers felt it to be their duty to suppress it, if possible. After orders forbidding gambling had been issued, the men would slip out and throw dice by moonlight. One night a little squad of guards were taken out of camp and deployed as skirmishers, and three or four soldiers were caught who had been gambling. Digging stumps was the penalty. How strict regulations, army discipline and full rations developed this disposition to gamble, is something it is not the province of the writer hereof to account for. The fact is simply stated.

While we were at Dechard, about the 1st of August, 1863, Col. Hull was detailed to act as a member of the Board to examine applicants for positions as officers of colored troops. The Board was located at Nashville, Tenn., and he went to the duty assigned him. This left Lieutenant-Colonel Ward in command of the Regiment. Col. Hull never returned to the Regiment, and Col. Ward commanded it till it was discharged by reason of expiration of time of service. I may be permitted to say that few, if any Colonels, retired from the service so generally esteemed and liked by the men of their Regiments as did Col. Ward. It must be a comfort to him in his old days to know that his comrades regarded, and still regard him, as pure, just, impartial and sufficiently brave to have gone with them to certain death if duty required it. We left this camp the 17th of August, and marched on the railroad to Cowan Station, a few miles distant. There we crossed the Cumberland mountain. All filled their canteens in the afternoon before they started up, and marched hard and steadily till dusk, when the top was reached. The next day we descended on the other side, and returned to the railroad at the point where the train, which carried many of our Regiment, was fired on Sept. 1st, 1862, nearly one year before. The Regiment went into camp on the evening of the 18th, near a place where a part of the Regiment had guarded bridges and water tanks for several weeks a year before. Notwithstanding the strict orders against leaving camp without a permit, some of the men did leave, and were gone some time in search of "the girl they left behind them" when they left there a year ago. Some of the boys reported progress when they returned, and we are informed some of them afterwards married the girls when "the cruel war was over." But this is only hearsay, and, if true, there was no wrong done.

While on this march many men were greatly troubled with diarrhœa, and the Colonel, fearing for their health, demanded that they should eat sparingly of the green corn. He told Dr. J. R. Goodwin—regimental surgeon, and a noble man, what he had done, and was informed by him that he had made a mistake; that the men needed vegetables. The Colonel told the men to eat all they could, which they did and recovered rapidly.

While marching toward our destination about the 20th of August, the Regiment halted one day for dinner, and remained there till the next day, a fine corn-field being on our right. On the left was a steep mountain, which nothing could climb. The road wound around the foot of this mountain, and on the right of the road

was a fence and corn-field. The guns were stacked in
the middle of the road, and at night the men slept at the
edge of the road on either side of their guns. There
was no fear of any enemy, and the sleep was sound and
sweet. But about midnight the wildest, most alarming
shrieks and shouts were heard in the distance that
the Thirty-seventh had ever heard. The trouble came
nearer and nearer, and now the awful and heaven-
defying profanity and blasphemy of the excited men,
the falling of gun-stacks and the heavy breathing and
snorting and jumping of a heavy animal were alarming,
indeed. Some sprang for their guns, some from them,
and in doing so seriously hurt themselves on rocks.
One man actually climbed a tree. On came the animal,
running over men and knocking down gun-stacks.

It was a large steer that had walked in at the rear
of the Regiment and moved on quietly till it tramped on
a sleeping soldier, who kicked, of course, and set the
animal going over men and stacks of guns, and got the
most soundly cursed of any man or beast in the Southern
Confederacy. It had to run the entire length of the
Regiment before it escaped, as the mountain was on one
side of the road and the fence on the other. After it
was gone the men laughed and cursed and scolded, and
then like good soldiers, laid down again. Some of the
men were hurt quite badly by jumping while half asleep
against the large rocks that had fallen from the ledges
above, but so far as is known none of them draw pensions for wounds received there, and this may be some
comfort to those who are so distressed about the soldiers
getting pensions.

Our last camp before we crossed the Tennessee river
was near the last of August. It was uncomfortably cold
here for several nights. While at this camp we were
called into line to witness the punishment of two artillery-

men, who, for some offense, had the hair shaved off of one side of their heads, and marched in front of the entire Brigade with a fifer before them playing "Poor, old soldier," and a file of soldiers behind them with bayonets fixed in distressingly close proximity to their seats. These same soldiers were conspicuous in the battle of Chickamauga in less than a month after that time, where they did their duty well.

They concealed from those who did not belong to the Brigade the evidence of the disgraceful punishment which had been inflicted on them by their officers for some offense, by tying up their heads in white cloth as if they were sore. It looked strange to see men who had so recently been so humiliated by their government's officers fighting so bravely for that government.

It was very apparent that the crime for which they had been punished was not cowardice. The way they fought in that hell of fire and smoke proved them to be good, true and brave American citizens.

John H. Brown, Co. A, wounded Sunday morning of the Chickamauga battle, Greensburg, Ind.

CHAPTER NINE

The Chickamauga Campaign—Crossing the River, Sand and Lookout Mountain—Skirmishing and Fighting—Pigeon Mountains—The Great Battle of Chickamauga.

About the last of August, 1863, a forward movement was ordered. We reached the Tennessee river a few miles below Stevenson the 1st day of September in the evening, and crossed the river on a pontoon bridge about midnight.

The Tennessee river is wide, and though it was midnight, the bright shining moon made everything look nicer, more romantic than if all had been lighted by the King of day. A man was in each little skiff on which the bridge rested to bail out the water. The mellow moonlight shining on the peaceful waters and shores of the river, made the brightly burnished rifles of the men and the swords of the officers look all the more terrible and out of harmony with the kind and gentle surroundings of nature. The putting of a great river behind us as we went farther into the enemy's country, increased the danger. But we were soldiers, and these thoughts

H. J. Steward, Co. A.
Letts' Corner, Ind.

were soon put out of mind. We all got over in good order and slept soundly on the Southern shore till morning. Then we marched a few miles up the river to a place where we were to cross Sand mountain.

We rested at the foot of that mountain till next morning, the 3d, and then started up it. The mountain was steep and the road villainous. The Thirty-seventh Ind. was distributed along the road at steep and rough places on the mountain and assisted the teams over it. The men had long ropes which they would fasten to each side of a wagon and fifteen or twenty men would pull on each of these ropes, and thus enable the mules to move the wagon a short distance. These men would leave this wagon to comrades at that point and go back with their ropes for another wagon until all were taken over.

General Negley, to whose division the Thirty-seventh belonged, not only supervised this work, but actually pulled off his coat and pulled at the ropes. While going up this mountain a sutler had stalled and worked his wagon out to the side of the road, and concluded to lighten his load by selling his goods at prices much higher than the mountain. Some of the boys were not pleased with his prices, and getting into a quarrel with him, tumbled his wagon, goods and everything down the mountain side. We slept on the mountain top that night, and the next day, the 5th, marched down its eastern slope into Lookout valley, and camped near Trenton Gap. The next day was the Sabbath, and we rested all day—blessed day of rest.

On the morning of the 7th we moved up the valley some distance. We were nearing the crossing of the fourth great barrier that we had to overcome during that campaign—the Cumberland mountain, the Tennessee river, Sand mountain, and last and greatest of all,

Lookout mountain. The 8th and 9th were spent in crossing the mountain, working part of the 9th digging great rocks out of the road and rolling them down the mountain side. Here, too, the men had to help haul the army wagons and artillery up the mountain. Finally the division (Negley's), got down the mountain, into McElmore's Cave. The Thirty-seventh was deployed as skirmishers on the 10th, and moved forward quite rapidly about a mile when it struck the enemy, and skirmishing began immediately.

The Thirty-seventh was supported by its Brigade and drove the enemy south on the Lafayette road toward Dug Gap. Perhaps the Thirty-seventh, and the division to which it belonged, never was in a more dangerous condition than just at that time. Nothing but the blundering of Gen. Bragg saved it from capture, as the whole rebel army of 45,000 men, who had fallen back from Chattanooga to that point, was in front of us An anecdote, told by a Confederate soldier to the writer of this since the war, shows that the Confederate soldiers who had "fallen back" with Bragg from Murfreesboro to Chattanooga, had become disgusted with him. After Bragg had fallen back to Chattanooga he joined the Episcopal church.

The next day after he had joined, a Confederate soldier said to another one: "Well, old Bragg joined church yesterday." "The old fool," said the other. "Oh," said the first speaker, "he wants to get to heaven just as bad as you do." "Of course he does," said the other, "but if he should get to heaven he would fall back the next day."

Bragg intended to capture that division of the army and then destroy or capture Crittenden and McCook in detail, but he was a little too slow. We had driven the enemy some miles when they made a stand. From some prisoners captured that day it was learned that we were in front of the entire Confederate army commanded by Gen. Bragg. Our whole force at that time consisted of three Brigades of Infantry, three Batteries and one Regiment of Cavalry, all commanded by Gen. Negley. That night the boys ate roasting-ears gathered from corn-stalks from twelve to fifteen feet high. The mountains kept the air cool and made vegetation late. We held our ground the 10th all day, skirmishing sharply at times. Those who were not on picket slept well that night. Leroy Roberts, of Co. F, was on picket that night and says: "The words of caution I received from the officer of the guard that night convinced me, boy that I was, that some one, high in authority, knew more than he cared to tell."

Leroy Roberts,
Dillsborough, Ind.

History informs us that at 9:30 that night Negley sent a message to Gen. Baird, who was following us with the first division, that he had encountered a large force of the enemy, and asked him if he would be up in time to assist him on the 11th. This dispatch was sent from the house of the widow Davis, near Chickamauga creek. We were in close quarters, indeed, and had Bragg's orders been carried out, the division would have been captured on the morning of the 11th; but their delays was their misfortune and our salvation. On the morning of the 11th a strong force in our front developed our position, and when they had done that they sent a strong force around our left flank. Their line of march could easily be seen by the great cloud of dust they raised. Baird had arrived, and with his Brigade it was necessary for the enemy to approach us cautiously.

While falling back, and still near Dug Gap, a woman carrying a little baby came out of a little white frame house over which bullets and shells were flying pretty thick. She spoke to no one, but started to the rear. Just as some one remarked "She runs like a deer," a deer jumped up and started after her; but whether it overtook her or not is not certain, for both disappeared in a thicket. After the Regiment had got back to a place of some safety, Co. B, of the Thirty-seventh, was sent back to Bridgeport for supplies, and returning Sunday, the 20th of September, struck McCook's corps rushing back demoralized, and was carried with it back to Chattanooga, and thus was kept, greatly to its regret, from participating in the great battle of Chickamauga.

Negley showed both courage and good generalship that day. While the rebels were really in our rear and front, he managed to keep a Brigade in front of them all the time. That was one of the most tiresome days the Thirty-seventh ever experienced. From early morning till after dark it was falling back, and taking positions, and marching to the flanks, and skirmishing with overwhelming numbers. And oh, how hot it was!

The men were nearly worn out moving from place to place, though Negley's presence and voice encouraged them greatly. About 3 o'clock in the afternoon, Hindman's gun on our left and rear, which was the signal for Bragg to attack us in front, was heard. The signal came too late to be of any advantage to the enemy. Just about this time, as the Thirty-seventh was standing in line of battle, Gen. George H. Thomas rode slowly up looking as peaceful and calm as the summer sky, inspiring all with new hope and courage, and causing many to say: "There's Pap Thomas, boys, it's all right now." Great and good and able Gen. George H. Thomas; without a peer in that army. We continued falling back slowly till we came to the mountain which protected our flanks, and there we rested and held the enemy at bay all night and next day. The Dug Gap campaign was a tiresome and dangerous one. The Thirty-seventh had several men wounded on the 10th and 11th, but none killed.

On the 11th, as we were falling back with the Confederate army as close after us as it was safe for them to come, we passed a small, but neat little frame house. One of our Batteries was firing at the advancing enemy, and one of their guns was firing at us. A shell from the enemy's gun struck the corner of the house, and, exploding, tore out the end of the building. A tall, and rather a nice looking lady came out with a large bible under her arm, and said to the boys in blue: "I hope, gentlemen, you will be highly entertained to-day, and I am glad to say the prospect for it is exceedingly bright," and she hurried on toward a place of safety.

On the 10th, Thomas McGuinness, of Co. K, was slightly wounded, and on the 11th, as we were hurrying through a corn-field to our left, a corn-stalk caught the hammer of some one's gun, causing it to explode, wounding Sergeant Jasper Plow, of Co. K, on the wrist so as to permanently disable him. He was a good and brave man. On the 11th we crossed the head waters of Chickamauga creek—a sluggish, nasty stream. It did not enter into our minds that soon we, with other Regiments, would make that little, insignificant stream famous the world over, and that on its banks thousands of the soldiers of the Union would pour out their blood for their government. On the 12th the other three divisions of our corps came rapidly down the mountain and joined us, and then we felt that with that position we could hold our own against the combined force of the enemy.

The Thirty-seventh remained near there till the 18th, when we moved by the left flank some miles north. After dark we took up our line of march again toward the north, and to what proved to be the bloody field of Chickamauga.

How far we marched that night I do not know, but we were going all night, sometimes I think in one direction and sometimes in another. The army seemed badly mixed, but I suppose it was all right. Fences were burning everywhere we went. Troops were passing all night and taking position on the left. Negley's division relieved Vandever the latter part of that night. Our Brigade laid down near the morning of the 19th to sleep, and was awakened by cannonading on our left. We watched the shells bursting and heard the cannons roar. Thomas was at Kelley's house, near the Lafayette road, confronting Bragg's army near Chickamauga

About noon the battle raged fiercely. McCook's division, tired and covered with dust, passed us going in the direction of the fighting. We lay there listening to the roar of artillery and the sharp rattle of musketry. Sometime in the afternoon Saturday, Negley was ordered to move in the direction of the battle. He started promptly, and after going some distance we came to Crawfish springs. There we were permitted to fill our canteens, which we gladly did, as we knew the importance of water in a battle. What a beautiful spring of water that was, and is! Think of going from that pure life-giving fountain of clear, cold water, springing up in great abundance, to a great and dreadful battle where smoke and dust and toil and wounds and death hold high carnival. That is war. Negley seemed anxious to get into the fray—seemed vexed at the deliberation of some of the men when drinking the water or filling their canteens. But that was the last quiet or water that we got till Sabbath night after the battle. Near the Lee house was Rosecran's headquarters before moving to the widow Glenn's. We moved forward rapidly and soon began to meet wounded men and stragglers—many were badly wounded and many were only scared—stampeded. This was an unusual sight to the Thirty-seventh, but something that may always be seen at the rear of a great army engaged in battle.

As we marched through an open field our army lay at the edge of a woods some sixty rods in front of us. We saw our line for a distance of nearly a quarter of a mile in length and it was firing as fast as it could. The wounded were coming back in great numbers, and W. C. Patton, of Co. K, asked one of them how they were making it in front. He said: "Well, it's about nip and tuck and d—d if I ain't afraid tuck has the best of it." Others though badly wounded, said they were getting along all right.

Sergeant Lafayette Ford, Co. E. Detroit, Mich.

We went on, passed the widow Glenn's house—Rosecran's headquarters. We were on the dry valley road, and still west some distance of the fighting line. We went, I am told, to the west and north of Brothertons, and formed our line of battle and the men laid down. While there an officer rode up and asked what Regiment that was. No one answering promptly, Rufus

Hudelson, of Co. K, jumped up, and in the most cheerful tone of voice, said: "The Thirty-seventh Indiana, and we only have one more year to serve." Nothing could have been more ridiculous than to be delighted that we only had one year of that kind of fighting to do. About dark severe fighting began on our left, and we were ordered forward into a woods. It was very dark and the ground had been fought over, and many guns were lying on the ground. We could see the fire leaping from the guns of our soldiers on our left, and hear the bullets of the enemy whizzing past, but there was no fighting at our front, and we had only one man wounded. Thus it is in war. Sometimes we plunge into danger when we little expect it, and sometimes when we think we are marching into the jaws of death, the battle lifts and no one is hurt. At times when the battle is raging at its fiercest, all in a few minutes will become as quiet as any Sabbath morning. We made

David H. Hair, Co. F,
Elrod, Ind.

temporary fortifications there of logs and rails, and laid down to rest. The night was dark and cold, and the groans of the wounded in our front added to the gloomy surroundings. Thirty-seventh men carried back many poor, wounded rebels that night and cared for them as best they could.

Before all the wounded were cared for, the queen of the night arose in all her splender and lighted up the blood-stained field with her cold rays. Col. Ward at the time quoted the words: "'Twas a calm, still night, and the cold, round moon looked down on the dead and dying." The night was cold, and the men suffered greatly, their clothing being wet with perspiration. They were not permitted to take their blankets from their knapsacks, and were compelled to lie on the cold ground shivering till the sun arose and warmed them with its heat. No heavier frost was ever seen than lay that morning on the battle field of Chickamauga. The moaning of the wounded had ceased the morning of the 20th as the sun arose above the hills, and many soldiers slept that sleep that knows no waking.

We gathered logs and rails out of which we made temporary breast-works, and waited for the battle to begin. A stiller Sabbath morning than that 20th morning of September was never known. The silence was oppressive. The firing of a few guns of either army would have been a relief. The sun climbed high up the steep of the heavens. About 9 o'clock we could hear the artillery wagons of the enemy moving toward our left. We all knew what that meant. About that time General Garfield and staff rode along the line a short distance in the rear. Soon after a rifle was heard, then another, and in a moment many others, and now many cannons on both sides are making the very earth shake with their awful roar. The battle was on in earnest. Rebel skirmishers try our line, but are easily repulsed. This was about 9:30 o'clock in the morning.

About 10 o'clock we, Sirwell's Brigade, was ordered to the support of Thomas, Beatty and Stanley's Brigades having preceded us. We went about a half mile when an order came to change front and retake our old position, which we did. From this point Col. Ward sent his horse back, which was captured by some Confederate Cavalry. We were again ordered to the left and rear to a hillside sloping towards the woods we left. We had

hardly formed our line when the Confederate line of battle advanced, but was soon halted by our artillery opening on them. The enemy then trained their artillery on us, but did no serious injury. Cannon balls tore through the timber and shells burst over our heads, but struck no one in our Regiment. Splinters knocked from trees by cannon balls struck Col. Ward and others, but hurt no one seriously.

At this point we discovered that the Thirty-seventh Indiana and the Twenty-first Ohio had become separated from the other Regiments of the Brigade. After staying a short time at this point we were ordered to the left by Gen. Negley. In obeying this order we crossed quite a little hill, and formed in an open woods. Shells were screaming through the tree tops, bursting over our heads and making a fearful noise, but doing but little harm. After standing there a short time we were ordered forward. The roar of battle was deafening, and we were sure we were going into it. We took position near a straw stack. Union troops on our right and a little in advance were in a corn-field, and the dust raised in the field by rebel bullets striking the ground among them, reminded one of the dust raised sometimes by a dashing summer's rain. It did not seem possible that we would get out of that place without fighting. The battle raged furiously on our right, while comparative quiet reigned in our front. A Union battery at our rear and on a hill, kept up a continual firing over us, and a rebel gun in our front was shooting over our heads at our battery it seemed. We remained at this place quite a while, but did no fighting and suffered no loss. A cannon ball from the rebel gun at our front struck a pine tree near the top some forty rods in front of us, tore through it, struck the ground in front of us, bounded against our breast-works of rails, and some of us think it rolled back, while others think it went on to the rear. From that position we were moved a short distance to the right and rear of the straw stack, and up a little hill near a house where a Union battery was firing very rapidly. This place seemed like a veritable hell; the blue smoke from the cannons' mouths made it difficult to see, and the roar was simply deafening. While at this place an officer rode up on a fiery steed flecked with foam and inquired "What Regiment is this?" On being told, he ordered us to charge over the point of the hill and capture a rebel Brigade.

Rufus Hudelson said: "I don't want any rebel Brigade." It was at that time, and is yet believed by many of us, including the writer of this, that that man was a rebel officer. Such things did occur on that day. To the right of us about 400 yards on that same hill the Ninth Indiana Regiment was fighting. The day was far gone and the smoke of battle hung on the moist air of evening. A rebel officer rode up to the Ninth and said: "Surrender, men; you are surrounded, and to fight longer is murder." Two men of the Ninth Indiana turned around and said: "Who the h—l are you?" and shot him off his horse. As he fell he said: "Oh, boys, why did you kill me?" Judge McConnel, of Logansport, was there and vouches for the truth of this. Both sides fought desperately there, for on the result of that battle the fate of the government seemed to hang.

Our Colonel had about finished the order to make the charge when an aid of Gen. Negley rode up and ordered us to move off by the right flank toward the rear. That we were at this time at the northern point of Snodgrass hill there is no doubt. I have been there three times since the battle, and think I cannot be mistaken about it. The hill and surroundings look quite natural. Comrade Leroy Roberts, of Co. F, visited that battle field while old man Snodgrass still lived in that house, and he told Mr. Roberts that the straw stack at which we formed our line as before stated, was undoubtedly his. The Twenty-first Ohio of our Brigade, the only Regiment of our division excepting the Thirty-seventh that was left on the field, was in the hottest of the fight on that hill.

We marched back and down a sloping hill through an open woods. In this open woods were artillery teams hitched to their wagons without riders, running wildly through the woods hauling the cannons. Some of the horses were shot and unable to travel and were dragged along. Men and officers by the scores were running wildly to the rear, seemingly having lost all pride and shame. Perhaps such a sight may always be seen in the rear of a great army engaged in battle, but it was a curious, uncommon and painful sight to the men of the Thirty-seventh Indiana Regiment. Col. Ward and the other officers of the Regiment acted wisely and fearlessly, and if there was any indication of fright among the men of the Thirty-seventh, I did not see it.

Our Regiment seemed so cool and orderly that I am told quite a number of men who were running away fell in with it, and for a time became a part of us. Our first stop was in an open field a half mile or more to the rear and north of Snodgrass hill, and on the road leading through McFarland's Gap, which is south of Rossville in the same Missionary ridge. We were ordered to the rear twice more that evening; the last time took us to or near Rossville, where we found Jeff. C. Davis rallying his troops. We were required to join him in that work, and gathered up quite a force, a number of them being without arms. The battle still raged with unabated fury at the front, and continued to do so till after dark.

We remained on the field near Rossville, and the firing at the front ceasing, laid down to rest and sleep. But thoughts of the dead and dying on that bloody battle ground greatly disturbed the rest of many who badly needed sleep. More than thirty thousand men had been killed or wounded in those two days, most of whom still remained where they fell. On the morning of the 21st, Gen. Negley rode up to us and inquired how the Indiana boys were at that time. The Thirty-seventh, after eating breakfast, was marched south some distance and placed on picket on Missionary ridge. The pickets were placed in little groups of three or four men some two or three rods apart. The rebels were anxious to know what we were doing and how strong we were, and about 3 o'clock p. m. sent out a scouting party to gain the desired information. They came a little too close, and Willis Vidito, of Co. F. killed one of them, and their curiosity was satisfied. We remained on that ridge all night—a long, cold, cheerless night, and at early dawn the 22d of September, we quietly came down the hill and marched into Chattanooga, the rebels following us so closely that their advance was in sight of us as we went into town, and the Chickamauga campaign was over, and Chattanooga, the objective point, was ours. Ours was the last Regiment to go into Chattanooga. The rebel Cavalry followed us pretty closely,

Willis Vidito,
Alsea, Oregon.

but showed no desire to attack us. Our army had the city—theirs the dead and wounded. Yet no campaign or battle of the war did greater honor to the fighting quality of the Northern soldiers, or accomplished more for the crushing of the rebellion than the battle of Chickamauga. When we arrived near Chattanooga the morning of the 22d, we faced to the front, went into camp, ate breakfast and prepared for the siege of Chattanooga.

CHAPTER TEN

The Siege of Chattanooga—Starving—Eating Corn, Cow Tails and Acorns.

J. W. Garrison, Co. H.
Greensburg, Ind.

Right good works had already been erected when we got into the town. Men were busy with picks and spades. Our pickets were out about a half mile south of our line. The enemy came on in force, attacked our pickets and seemed determined to bring on an engagement. Our Batteries opened on them that afternoon and a strong force started to re-inforce our pickets, and the attack was abandoned. All our energies were now put forth to strengthen the fortifications so that we could withstand any attack the enemy might make. A long trial of labor, exposure, danger and hunger was before the army, but it preferred almost anything to giving up the town. They had fought for it and got it, and would not surrender it now. Fortifying was seriously interrupted by the enemy's artillery. They kept up an almost incessant cannonading for several days, doing but little harm. One of the shells did not explode, and some colored men used one of them for an andiron. Soon there was a fearful explosion and one dead colored man and two or three seriously wounded. We worked the night of the 22d on Fort Negley. He told us if we would work well that night on the fort we need not fear anything the enemy could do.

We surely worked well all that night, and the guns of the Nineteenth Indiana Battery were put in position in that fort the morning of the 23d. The enemy did not seem anxious to try us again, and we continued fortifying. On the afternoon of the 23d we hoisted a flag on the fort and Negley said: "Now, let them come." but they did not. They were very provoking, never coming when we wanted them to, and generally coming when they were neither invited nor wanted. That may be some excuse for our using them so badly when they did come. Yet we would have treated them worse if they had come when we wanted them.

Marion Davis, Sergeant Co. B. Liberty, Ind.

Every available man was at this time put to work on the fortifications, and Chattanooga was fast becoming a well fortified city. The enemy continued to shell us, and make it very unpleasant and somewhat dangerous to work where shot or shells could reach us. The large gun they had on the top of Lookout mountain made a fearful noise, but did little harm, as they could not depress it enough to hit us by shooting directly at us without spoiling the carriage of the gun. Often they would shoot up so the ball would fall into our camp. This did no other harm to the Thirty-seventh, I believe, than to let a cannon ball drop through a dog tent in which Doc. Baker, of Co. G, was sitting reading. It tore a big hole in the tent, but did not touch him. One evening after we were pretty well fortified, the whole army, by common consent, I think, began cheering, and kept it up for half an hour.

The Thirty-seventh slept behind Fort Negley without any protection from the shot and shells of the enemy, or from the sun or rain or dew. Quite frequently at night when we were sleeping soundly, we would be aroused and hastily marched into Fort Negley. This was done that we might learn our position if we should be attacked.

It was at Fort Negley, and the 3d of October, that the enemy shelled us so vigorously all one afternoon. We had no protection, and the shot and shell came thick and fast. Their Batteries were in plain view, and only those who have experienced it can tell how slow time seems to fly while he is the target for an enemy's Battery. We expected a repetition of this shelling the next day, but did not get it. From this position we were soon removed to one at the foot of Cameron hill. They continued to shell us from Lookout mountain, but could not depress their gun enough to harm us much.

But worse than shot and shell were the short rations on which we were placed. The hard work and exposure to which we were subjected made full rations a necessity. Instead of this we were suddenly put on half rations, and much less than that. Thousands of men there for the first time felt the gnawing of hunger without knowing when or how it would be satisfied. Men would take the corn from the horses and mules, hundreds of which were starved to death. A dollar would willingly have been given for a five-cent loaf of bread. Where beeves were slaughtered, men would go out and cut the tails from the hide and bring them in and cook them. The weather was getting cold, and every tree inside of our lines was cut down for fuel. When all these were consumed, the stumps and roots of the trees were dug up and used for fuel.

This was a time of severe trial and suffering. Many became weak and emaciated, yet not one word was uttered about evacuating the city. "Hold it till clothing and provision comes" was the sentiment of all. I believe no army ever showed more patience, courage or patriotism than did that grand old army of the Cumberland. But relief came at last.

Hooker arrived with the Eleventh and Twelfth corps at Bridgeport and drove the enemy back to within a few miles of Chattanooga; and then a Brigade under Gen. Turchin was loaded in small boats at Chattanooga, and after dark they silently floated down the Tennessee river to a position held by the Confederates, from which they controlled it. It had rained the night before, and the rebels, seeing the little boats floating down, said: "See how the river is rising and floating down logs." Turchin's men landed and began fighting at once. The battle raged furiously from about 11 o'clock to 1, when the enemy gave up the position, leaving the field to Turchin. This gave us control of the river to within a mile of the city, and provision and ammunition were easily hauled from there.

Col. Hull returned some time in November and took command of the Regiment, and Col. Ward was detailed as a member of a court martial, which held its sessions in Chattanooga. On the 23d of November the members of the court martial were returned to their commands, and the Thirty-seventh moved near Fort Wood. We marched over the knoll through the camp of the Ninth Ohio, while the enemy's guns on Missionary ridge indicated trouble ahead. We slept that night in the rear of the trenches at the right of Fort Wood. The 24th was the battle of Lookout mountain, which we saw plainly from our position, and if a prettier sight was ever seen, the Thirty-seventh did not see it. Many able and gifted writers have attempted to describe it, but all failed. Consequently, I shall not try it. But the recollection of it makes us all glad that we were soldiers of the Union.

The next day, the 25th, was the battle of Missionary ridge. About 2 o'clock the army commenced moving as if on review. Confederate officers sitting on their horses at Bragg's headquarters on Missionary ridge were plainly seen, watching the movements of our army. It marched directly toward Orchard Knob, a high point held and fortified by the Confederates, about half way between the city and the ridge. When the leading division had come to within a few hundred yards of the knobs, the order was given to double quick, and the artillery to open fire.

When the command "Charge" was given, instantly the brave fellows went cheering as they went and never halted till they had driven the enemy from their fortifications. Some of the Thirty-seventh men helped to carry wounded men off the battle field the next day. Comrade Leroy Roberts assisted the next day in carrying an officer from the field who was hurt so badly that he did not speak.

The Thirty-seventh returned to its camp on the 27th of November. On the 28th we were ordered to make a reconnoissance on Lookout mountain, and started on the evening of the 29th, arriving on the top of the mountain about 9 o'clock at night. We went up on the government road. On the 30th we marched on top of the mountain south, and slept that night on the mountain top. Men in camp made fires out of pine knots which were numerous there. The pickets had no fires and suffered greatly from the cold.

The next day we returned to camp. Dec. 1st, I think. Our mission on the mountain was to see if the enemy was all off the mountain. I think they were. Before these battles the Thirty-seventh helped to fortify Cameron hill. Rations were short much of the time and often men went to bed hungry, and working on such rations was soldiering under difficulties. December passed slowly away—exceedingly slowly to soldiers who had been passing through such active service. Camp duty and guard duty were about all that broke the monotony of our camp life. Col. Ward was again detailed on a court martial, and continued on it till the last of December, when it was removed to Nashville, Tenn., the Colonel going with it.

The year 1863 is gone into history. And in the language of Comrade Roberts, "Its record of events will leave their imprint beyond the lapse of time." The New Year came in dull and cold, as all will remember that New Year's Day is called the "Cold New Year's."

The rations were very short, and it was almost impossible to obtain fuel. Roots were dug from the ground, the stumps having already been used. The suffering was severe the 1st and 2d. We drew a small ration of flour the 3d, which we cooked as best we could. It rained the 4th, and for the sake of appearance, with little of the reality, we drew tea—just a little. The 5th and 6th were colder, but not much. Two steamboats stopped at the landing the 7th, and then went on toward Knoxville. On the 8th there was a slight snow fall, and Capt. Shook was in command of the Regiment, and had inspection.

Our rations gave out on the 9th, and we passed the day in good condition physically and mentally to sympathize with the much-abused army mule which still refused to die. But rations came on the 10th, and we were all glad again, and ready to swear that Uncle Sam was a good provider, and that we would see him out of his trouble into which his bad brother had gotten him. We were still at Cameron hill, where we had often stood on dress parade and seen our battery on Moccasin point throw solid shot and bursting shell against the rocky top of Lookout mountain. The base of that mountain furnished us wood after the enemy left. A company that had an ax was well off, but old soldiers are great borrowers. Camp guard and dress parade were introduced again on the 12th. From this time to the 17th rations were scarce; boats were passing and re-passing, trains were coming and going, but rations came in slowly. On the 17th we received a marching order to go with four days' rations.

We left the 18th, with rain pouring down, going in a north-easterly direction, crossed the Chickamauga river, the Western, Atlanta and East Tennessee R. R. and camped within two miles of Harrison. Camped near the same place the next evening. A strong Union sentiment prevailed there. This was about twelve miles from Chattanooga, and near the Tennessee river. It snowed on the 19th. On the 21st we marched in an easterly direction, and passed a house that had the "old flag"—red, white and blue, hung out and floating proudly in the breeze. We stopped at a small town on the East Tennessee and Georgia R. R., five miles from Harrison and fifteen from Chattanooga, and finding no enemy, we marched back to Chattanooga, reaching there at 10 o'clock at night. Orders to move camp awaited us on our arrival. We struck tent the morning of the 22d, and moved to the right and front of Fort Wood, where we began housekeeping again.

We were not loth to leave this old camp. We had left many camps with feelings of sadness and sometimes apprehensions amounting to almost fear. A curious thing about soldier life is that one will sometimes become greatly attached to some camp after staying there but a few days. But that old camp we were willing to leave. There, from October till late in January, we had suffered hunger, cold and all the privations incident to soldier life, and we were rather glad to leave. Still, during the long siege, and the many battles in the meanwhile, the loss of life from all causes had been small. We were still on short rations, but knew this trouble could not last long. The next day, the 23d of January, we got our lumber and plunder from the old camp and fixed up our quarters, and for the first time in many, many days, drew full rations of flour.

The weather was favorable and that was a busy, merry, happy day for the boys of the Thirty-seventh Indiana. We spent the 24th also in improving our quarters, building mud chimneys and fire-places. Policing our camp and having dress parade were the duties imposed on us for some days. The weather was very fine and the general health of the Regiment good. About this time the question of re-enlistment, and a furlough was sprung on the old soldiers. That was at that time the common subject of conversation in the army. "Re-enlist and get a furlough" was urged quite frequently. Details from the Regiment for work on the forts about the city on the 27th and 28th were made. The 30th the Regiment went to town to do fatigue duty, but returned without working. The 31st it rained till near evening.

February the 1st was nice, as most of the days had been for some time. We drilled on the 3d, and a detail worked on the fort under Lieut. Sage. The 4th and 5th passed without interest, and a detail went on picket on the 6th under Lieut. Tevis. That was a disagreeable day. The 7th we saw the railway depot burn in town, and on the 8th we had dress parade, and on the 9th Battalion drill. Nothing of importance occurred till the 11th, when the Regiment signed the pay roll for two months' pay. Gen. Mansfield arrived on the 12th. His mission was to encourage the soldiers to re-enlist He addressed the Thirty-seventh on that subject the 12th of February. On the 13th Co. A re-enlisted as veterans.

Selecter Thackery, Co. D.
Ballstown, Ind.

We had dress parade in the evening, Capt. J. B. Reeve in command of the Regiment, he having recently been returned to the Regiment.

From this on to the 18th nothing unusual occurred excepting that it was getting colder. On the 19th a number of Co. F called on the writer, who had returned from Indiana, where he had been sent to recruit. He gave them a description of the land north that "flowed with milk and honey." On the 21st we received orders for a reconnoissance, which proved to be the campaign to Buzzard Roost and Dalton. At this time the Thirty-seventh Regiment was a part of the third Brigade of the first division of the fourteenth corps. Col. Hambright, of the Seventy-eighth Pennsylvania, commanded the Brigade, and Gen. R. W. Johnson commanded the division. It was nearly noon of the 22d when we started on the march, and we went on till night and camped near Ringold for the night. We knew nothing of where, or for what we were going.

We passed through Ringold the morning of the 23d. We had not gone far before our cavalry began skirmishing with the enemy. The fighting was kept up all day, sometimes rising to the dignity of a battle. That night we camped near Tunnel hill, at which place the enemy was strongly fortified. We picketed the left flank of our army that night. On the morning of the 24th our pickets were attacked by the enemy's cavalry, but our army marched on as if nothing were opposing it.

It soon became apparent that we had found a strong force of the enemy. They had a battery posted on an eminence in our front, which they handled with consummate skill. The firing was too fierce for the cavalry, and as they retired the infantry took their place. We were in the highway and had to move

Capt. G. W. Meyer, Co. I. Chattanooga, Tenn.

out into the timber for shelter, and to conceal our movements from the enemy. One of the enemy's shells struck under the horse (a white one) of Gen. Whipple, chief of staff of Gen. Thomas, before we got into the woods. The noise of the artillery and musketry was equal to that of a real battle, yet our loss was slight, as the place was easily taken by a flank movement. That night we slept in the old rebel camp, and warmed ourselves by fires made from material they had gathered

On the 25th we heard heavy firing in our front, and pushed forward with all possible speed. By night our army had driven the enemy back to Buzzard Roost Gap in front of Dalton, Ga. This gap was an impregnable position against any attack from the front. It is situated in Rocky Face ridge, 1,000 feet high, through which Mill creek, a small stream, runs; also the Western and Atlanta railroad. This was Gen. Johnston's bulwark in May following, and which Sherman, with his army of 120,000, had to flank by passing through Snake Creek Gap several miles south.

The Twenty-fourth Illinois on the 24th was in front, commanded by the gallant Col. Mihilotzy. He requested that the Thirty-seventh Indiana support him as he assaulted the enemy's position, which it did, Capt. Hezekiah Shook, of Co. D, being in command. Two Companies of the Thirty-seventh—D, commanded by Lieut. Hunt, of Co. K, and K, commanded by Capt. J. B. Reeve, were thrown forward as advance pickets of the other Companies of the Thirty-seventh. It was dark as we approached the foot of a spur of the high hill. The enemy was on this spur in force, and while Col. Mihilotzy was establishing his line near it he was mortally wounded. He fell and died there. Companies K and D made breast-works of logs and rails, close to the rear of the Twenty-fourth Illinois, and the remainder of the Thirty-

Lieut. W. R. Hunt, Co. K.
Treaty, Ind.

seventh lay some considerable distance in our rear. We dare not take out our blankets, or remove our accouterments all night. We lay and shook and shivered, with the ground freezing around us all night, and wondered if the Johnnies would not freeze before day in their cotton summer clothes. But they amused themselves all night shooting at us at distressingly short range—sometimes firing by files, and sometimes by volleys. We suppose they had a great deal of fun that night, and that none of them froze.

The eight Companies of the Thirty-seventh that were in our rear fell back a few hundred yards some time in the night, and Companies D and K, a considerable distance apart, held their positions till daylight.

The Twenty-fourth Illinois, which was a short distance in our front, was very close to the enemy, and quiet since the death of their Colonel. Sometime before day the enemy opened a fearful fire on them and us. We could see the fire leaping from their guns, and hear the bullets whizzing past our heads. This stampeded the Twenty-fourth, and they came back pell mell, some of them running right over our works. James Hall, of Co. K, was sitting behind our little works with his left hand holding his gun, which was leaned against the works, while he gazed intently at the front. A Twenty-fourth man running back with all his might, and not seeing us or our breast-works, fell over it upon Hall's arm and lay there. "Jim" never looked at him, but taking him by the collar with his right hand, threw him to the rear as if he had been a cat. Some little time after this the rebels opened a furious fire again, and we felt sure they would charge us.

Capt. Reeve told us to hold our fire till they got close to us, but none did it but myself. I saw a large fellow coming down the hill through the bushes as if determined to be the first man to demand our surrender. Our men were re-loading their guns, and when he got close enough I aimed and fired, and saw the man I shot at spring and stagger to one side into the thick bushes, and as he did so his blue uniform showed out clearly. I knew that I had shot a Union soldier—a Twenty-fourth Illinois man, and my heart sank within me. After that for a time I took little interest in what was going on. But I was sure that no one but myself knew what I had done, and I determined to tell no one. Sometime in the afternoon we learned that a Twenty-fourth Illinois man had been wounded in the foot as he was coming off the field that morning.

To have heard that the war was over would have given me no more pleasure than did that news. I never knew that anyone knew what I had done till some three weeks afterwards. Capt. Reeve said to me one day: "Well, Puntenney, you came pretty nearly getting that Dutchman." He said he saw it all, but thought it best to say nothing about it at the time. I sincerely hope he got well and is now drawing a large pension for the disability he received while in the discharge of his duty in vigorously conducting a masterly retreat from the most dangerous place a man ever occupied. But to return to the Companies, D. and K.

Capt. Reeve sent Newton Cowan to the rear to inform our commander of our position, and for orders. He returned and reported that the Regiment was gone. The Captain then sent him to Col. Hambright—to Brigade headquarters. He returned with orders to fall back to our Regiment, which the two Companies did without the loss of a man. We went back about half a mile, I think, and lay there all day. The Nineteenth Illinois kept up a pretty fierce fight on the left side of the gap all afternoon, and got several men killed and wounded. Orders were given to fall back quietly after dark, and Co. K was given the position of rear guard. After dark the army began to move back, making no noise but that made by the artillery wagons, and it seemed that they made more noise that soft, balmy night, than common.

Co. K formed across a narrow place between the hills through which the road leading back ran. The men were standing about twenty feet apart facing the enemy, waiting till the army would get a good start. While waiting we could hear trains arriving at Dalton and unloading soldiers. We could hear them laugh and talk just as we had done many times. They asked where we were, and how many of us there were, saying they would clean us out to-morrow. About 9 o'clock the moon arose in all its splendor, and we were still standing there, and no enemy appearing to follow our army, we were ordered to fall back and join our command, which we did.

The moon shone brightly and it seemed that all nature was at rest, and we were at ease. A great many good men had lost their lives the day and night before, and I am now pained to say that that did not greatly distress us. We were soldiers, and acted as such.

We marched on till about midnight feeling perfectly secure, when suddenly the roar of a cannon was heard in our rear. The enemy had learned of our departure and were following us, but the cavalry kept them at a respectful distance. They did nothing more than banter us by bragging about Chickamauga. We went into camp near Ringold, not fearing the enemy. We remained in camp the next day—the 27th, until about noon, when we started on our return trip, and arrived at our destination, Tyner's Station, that evening, some twenty miles from Buzzard Roost.

Tyner Station is a small village on the Tennessee and Georgia R. R. The morning of the 28th we established our camp on the high ground near the village. The weather had been nice for some days, but on the 1st of March it rained, turning cold. On the 2d, the Fifteenth corps passed our camp moving east, on their way to Cleveland. We fixed up nice quarters there and made ourselves quite comfortable. The weather was nice until the 6th, when the pay-master arrived. For several days veteran troops who had been home on veteran furlough were returning. It was quite rainy from the 7th to 15th. In the meantime we were picketing, guarding and doing camp duty. Companies B, C and D having veteranized, marched to Chattanooga the 14th, where they received transportations home on a thirty days' furlough.

The Twenty-first Ohio returned the 14th, having been home on furlough. Co. I returned the 15th (a cold day), having been home on a veteran furlough. We received marching orders the 18th with two days' rations, and started on the 19th and arrived at our destination, Graysville, Ga., distant from Tyner's Station about six miles. We went into camp on a gently sloping hillside near the village. Graysville was then and is yet a small place—a mere station. While on this march Lieut. Speer, who had been home on a recruiting furlough, joined us. At Tyner's we made our tents quite comfortable. It was warm and when not on guard duty we slept nicely. On the 22d we were ordered to march with two days' rations to Parker's Gap for picket duty. Parker's Gap is a defile in the White Oak mountains, and about six miles from Tyner's Station.

When we got up on the morning of the 22d we found fully ten inches of snow on the ground, and snow still falling rapidly. After a very poor breakfast we started to the gap, going nearly all the way through a pine woods. The small pines were bent by the weight of the snow till their tops in many cases touched the ground. All were heavily burdened with snow. Shake one of them ever so slightly as you went under it, and an avalanche of snow would fall down on you, causing you to feel very uncomfortable. The march, with all the accouterments which a soldier needed at that time of the year, through that deep snow, was very tiresome. We finally arrived at our destination, placed our pickets out and scraped the snow off the ground where we intended to sleep when night came. A less inviting place for sleeping than that was is seldom seen even by a soldier. The only good thing that could be truthfully said of the place was, "there were no graybacks there." We gathered wood, built fires and dried the ground where we slept that night. The next morning we reconnoitered the gap in the mountain but found no enemy. The Twenty-first Ohio relieved us on the 24th and we returned to our camp and had a good sleep. It rained and snowed the next day and made it necessary for us to ditch around our quarters. We had dress parade on the 27th, Capt. Hughes in command of the Regiment. On the 28th we went again to Parker's Gap with five days' rations. Nothing of any importance occurred while there. We remained there till April 1st, when we returned to camp at Graysville.

About the only duty we had at Graysville was police duty, guard duty and an occasional scout, with more or less company drill. Veterans were returning from their furloughs, and had brought some of the sports and vices of civil life with them and introduced them into camp. Cards and dice and novel reading were discarded for home fun. That was dancing. All the spare time most of the men had, especially in the evenings, was devoted to dancing. Nearly every Company had one or more fiddlers, and "the sound of music and dancing" was heard all along the line. All knew they were on the eve of starting on a campaign, the like of which had never been on the continent, and in which many of them would lay down their lives and lay mangled on bloody fields of battle, yet they danced as merrily as if they had been at home in time of profound peace. Man is a curious creature. On the 16th of April we had regimental inspection, Major Kimball in command, and dress parade in the evening. Sunday, the 17th, was a lovely day, and Col. Ward, who had been absent on a court martial, returned to the Regiment and was gladly welcomed back. On the next evening Col. Ward had dress parade again. We went to Parker's Gap again on the 20th, scouted for the enemy, but found none. Drilling and dress parade and inspections occupied much of our time during these days.

T. F. Brown, Co. B.
Cherryvale, Kas.

All understood that the campaign—the greatest, and it was hoped the last of the war, was about to be entered upon. The veteran Companies C and D returned the 30th of April. The 2d day of May we got orders to have two days' rations in our haversacks, and be ready to move at an hour's notice. On the 3d we marched in the direction of Ringold, Ga., crossed the East Chickamauga river and went into camp in the afternoon about a mile from Ringold. The situation there was inviting, and the desire to remain there, perhaps induced the men to fix up their quarters nice, indeed. The few days we remained there will be remembered as one of the really bright and happy times in the history of the Thirty-seventh Indiana. At that time we learned that the Thirty-eight Indiana had been transferred to our Brigade, and that Col. Scribner was our Brigade commander. All our division—the first, was assembled at this place and camped in this valley. The tents, all white and new, set up according to army regulations, presented a beautiful appearance indeed. Yet it all looked like war. For some time each Company had been drawing candles, and on the evening of the 6th we received orders to march.

T. B. Peery, Co. E.
Greensburg, Ind.

The men knew that meant that the campaign was on, and that they would need their candles no more. So some one in Co. A said he would illuminate with his candles. He cut his candle in pieces and brilliantly lighted his tent and surroundings. Others took up the thought, and in a few minutes every Company in the Regiment was burning their candles. I believe the craze extended throughout the division. The night was calm and men climbed trees and started pieces of candles to burning all over the tree tops. It is safe to say that 10,000 lights were burning at one time in the tree tops, making a most beautiful sight. Thousands of men yet living remember that grand sight and the enthusiasm it inspired. Hundreds of those poor fellows never saw another candle after that night. That was the last quiet day and night of that spring and summer, for the morrow, the 7th of May, ushered in the Atlanta campaign.

CHAPTER ELEVEN

The Atlanta Campaign—Buzzard Roost—Rocky Face—On to Resaca.

Early in the morning of May 7th we advanced with light hearts and firm steps toward the front. We passed through Hooker's Gap, on to Tunnel hill, which was occupied by a strong force of the enemy. We arrived at Tunnel hill about 3 o'clock p. m., on the 7th, but did not attack the enemy that night. The Fourteenth corps was in the center, Hooker on our right and Howard on our left. On the morning of the 8th the Thirty-seventh took a position on a hill fronting the enemy. A few hundred cavalrymen formed in a valley and moved forward first in a trot and then in a gallop. When they got some distance to the front the enemy's batteries opened on them, and of all the wild rides to the rear ever seen, that was the wildest.

The tramp of the fleeing horses' hoofs, the awful swearing, clanging of sabers and carbines, and the bursting of shells among the men and horses made a scene never to be forgotten. After remaining in that position a short time the Thirty-seventh moved around to the right, and the enemy, seeing they would be flanked, retired to Buzzard Roost.

Before leaving that position the enemy poured a hot fire on us, but did little harm. We followed the enemy to his stronghold on the 9th, skirmishing with his rear guard continually. We reached Buzzard Roost about the middle of the afternoon. The Thirty-seventh had been there before, and was placed in advance. Companies A and K, under Capt. J. B. Reeve, were deployed as skirmishers. We moved by right of Companies out of a field, crossed a creek with the other Companies close in our rear, into the thickest possible underbrush imaginable. It was a pine woods that had been burned over. The large trees were dead and the undergrowth of shrubbery very thick. As the enemy's shell tore through and burst among those old, dead tree tops, bringing down old limbs with a crash, we were almost ready to conclude that pandemonium reigned supreme. We were subjected to a severe fire from the enemy's batteries and rifles, but we never halted nor wavered. Shells burst over the heads of the men, and in one or two instances plowed through the Companies, but they caused no man to even falter. No soldiers in that charge were more, or even so much exposed as was the Thirty-seventh Regiment, and no Regiment acted more calmly and defiantly than the Thirty-seventh. One felt that it was a real honor to be associated with such a body of strong, daring and loyal men.

Gen. Johnson in his official report says five assaults on Rocky Face ridge were repulsed on the 9th day of May. The assault of the Thirty-seventh was made on that day and it was not repulsed. Its men slept on the ground that night, protecting themselves as best they could from sharp shooters, and a battery on Rocky Face over to the left Perhaps this battery was one mile away, yet it could land and explode its shells in our very midst. Some Ohio Regiment was taking position on our right and the enemy shelled them as they were doing so. As the flash from the cannon was seen away on the top of Rocky Face, the officers of that Regiment would all shout, some saying, "Here she comes, boys!" Others, "Steady, steady, boys!" And just then the shell would fly screaming over our heads and burst near that Regiment. I do not know how many men that Regiment lost. The Thirty-seventh had several men severely wounded, and a few killed.

The enemy was concealed from our view and we did not have the poor satisfaction of shooting at them. It took courage to receive the fire of the enemy and have no opportunity of returning it, but the Thirty-seventh had that courage. We lay there all night, and, strange to say, slept pretty well. Co. F supported the pickets that night, and were relieved on the 10th by Co. I. The skirmish line was advanced on the 10th, during which the Regiment lost two men. There was brisk fighting in the evening, and it rained hard that night. During the 11th we built rail and log breast-works and skirmished sharply all day. On the evening of the 11th we were relieved by Stanley's division—Fourth corps, and marched to the rear.

The next morning, the 12th, we, with the rest of the army, started for the right and marched through Snake Creek Gap, a narrow defile through Rocky Face ridge. It was getting dark as we emerged into a valley on the east of the ridge, near Resaca and the railroad at the rear of the Confederate army. It was night and dark when the Thirty-seventh went into camp that night on a high mound or nole. On the morning of the 13th as we awoke and looked over that valley from our elevation the grandest sight and the most unexpected was witnessed that was ever seen on the continent.

We did not know that nearly the whole army had marched into that valley before us. But it had. There were 90,000 men with flags and banners floating in the balmy breeze of that bright spring morning; Regiments of Cavalry feeding; scores of brightly burnished cannons shining in the sunlight, and all the other strange things of a great army were before us. Looking at all these things brought to mind the scripture: "Fair as the moon, clear as the sun and terrible as an army with banners." Not many times on this earth has such a sight been presented to mortals as was that which the Thirty-seventh saw from its elevated position.

Johnson had fallen back to Resaca with his army of 70,000 men, according to his own report. He was strongly entrenched, having fortifications thrown up before he fell back to them. The Thirty-seventh having been in the rear the day before was placed in front the 13th and moved out slowly, having left our knapsacks where we had slept the night before.

The army was massed in that valley, and it took a long time to get to the front. Regiments—many of them, laid down and we walked over them. Finally we got out and entered a dense woods. The battle line where we were was three Regiments deep, the Thirty-seventh in the advance. It was Thursday, and about 10 o'clock in the morning when we started forward, going, I think, in a northeasterly direction. About noon, or a little after, our skirmishers began firing an occasional shot. As we moved forward the skirmishing became brisker, but not very fierce. That night we were relieved and took our position on the rear line. Gen. Kirkpatrick was wounded on the 13th.

We supported Carlin's Brigade on the 14th. He advanced rapidly, and the skirmishing grew in fierceness until it developed into a battle. That was the first real fighting at Resaca. A goodly number of wounded men were carried back through our lines to the rear. Poor fellows! Some of them looked pale from loss of blood and pain, but I do not remember of hearing one of them utter a word or even a moan. They were carried on stretchers which were soaking wet and fiery red with patriots' blood. While this was going on and we were standing in line of battle, we heard of Grant's success at Spottsylvania. We moved to the left a little that evening and put up temporary breast-works. The battle raged fiercely all day the 15th, and neither side seemed to have much the best of it.

The left of our line of battle rested on, and north of the railroad, and the left of Johnson's army rested on the same road farther east. Trains of cars of the Union side arrived at our battle line in the midst of the fight bringing provisions and ammunition, and returning took wounded men off the field. Trains of the enemy did the same. When the whistle of our trains was heard, our soldiers would cheer and the rebels would cheer as their trains arrived. Saturday night, the 15th, we were moved in the darkness to another position. We laid down and slept, though it rained most of the night. In the morning, Sunday, the 16th, we found but a few poles for breast-works, and while trying to locate the enemy a solid shot went screaming over our heads. As we had no works and the enemy only two or three hundred yards from us, we hugged the ground as our best friend.

A Prussian Captain of a battery, who wore buckskin breeches and was called "Buckskin," called for his men to bring up a gun. Almost instantly six horses with a man on each near horse, attached to a cannon wagon, galloped furiously forward. In wheeling so as to point to the front the wheel struck a stump and turned over the cannon. Then another came and turned into position. It was shoved close to the brow of the hill and fired at the enemy's cannon. Rebel sharp shooters made it so dangerous to load the cannon that men had to crawl under the gun, and lying on their backs, load it. The Thirty-seventh men also got position as sharp shooters and did much toward keeping down rebel sharp shooters. In about two hours' time "Buckskin" had silenced the enemy's battery and we had but little to do that day but listen to minnie balls passing over our heads and to the roar of battle on our right and left.

About midnight the enemy, after opening up on us for a few minutes most furiously, and receiving a parting salute from our batteries, fell back across the Oostenaula river. And another battle had been fought, the enemy had been driven, but not defeated or even routed. Gen. Wilder says if Sherman had come to him as he should have done when he was in the rear of Resaca, Johnson might have been destroyed, and it seems as if he were right. Resaca was a great battle, both armies losing considerably. Capt. Reeve and others went over to see what effect "Buckskin's" shots had on the rebel battery. They found there a disabled cannon, dead horses, not a few, and pieces of almost every part of the human body lying scattered on the ground. On our right our army had taken a position on a hill near Resaca, and the enemy charged it in the hope of gaining that position. Many dead Confederates lay there still on Monday. Several had reached the Union line of battle and were killed and buried under the earth that was thrown up for works while they continued to fight, only their feet and legs being uncovered. More than forty bullets struck a large pine tree just at the rear of Co. K that day. On the morning of the 17th we passed through Resaca and crossed the Oostanaula river and followed Johnson on toward Calhoun.

CHAPTER TWELVE

Our Army Moves Forward to Calhoun Battle of Pumpkinvine.

J. H. Connelly,
New Point, Ind.

No time was lost or rest taken. We pressed forward rapidly, meeting many prisoners who were being sent to the rear. The advance of Howard's corps kept up a lively skirmish with the rear of the enemy. On the 18th we stopped beyond Calhoun for dinner at a place where they said Johnson ate his breakfast.

We marched through Adamsville with drums beating and flags unfurled to the breeze—marched till late at night, and camped in an open field near Kingston. About noon the 16th we passed through Kingston, many prisoners still going to the rear. In the evening we moved to the left and built breast-works that night. The next morning we moved forward, passing the enemy's saltpetre works, and camped in an open field and threw up works. Nothing of note but picket firing and some cannonading occurred on the 20th, 21st and

22d. On the 23d, I think, we waded the Etawah river, a wide, beautiful stream, the water being about three feet deep. Beneath the surface of the water are many smooth stones standing at an angle of about thirty degrees and very slippery. The men hung their shoes and stockings and coats and pants on their bayonets and waded into the water.

Skirmishers were making it lively in the woods beyond the river, and the men being interested in that, paid little attention to their footsteps. Consequently, several men stepped onto a slick and slanting rock and disappeared beneath the water. Then if he knew any new oaths he delivered himself of them while his comrades laughed. Several times as a soldier laughed at the misfortune of another, he would step on a stone and go under the water and come out cursing to be laughed at just as the other had. There was more fun in crossing that river than is often experienced in an ordinary lifetime. If I am not greatly mistaken, it was at that time and that river that these duckings occurred.

Wm. H. Scott, Co. K, died June 20th 1895, Kingston, Ind.

We went on driving the enemy before us till the 25th, when the enemy made a determined stand, and Hooker, with all his dash and courage, could not drive him. The Thirty-seventh was in Hooker's rear during this engagement. Nothing of special interest occurred on the 26th. At midnight we were ordered to move,

and did so. About noon, or a little after, our whole division was massed in a large open field. After staying there a short time we made another advance.

We have now come to the battle of Pumpkinvine, sometimes called "Pickett's mills," because of an old grist mill just in the rear of our line of battle. I believe only our Brigade—Scribner's, was engaged in that battle. The Thirty-seventh was on the extreme left, and the enemy's right extended much beyond our left.

We moved noiselessly through a dense woods. Not a sound of war could be heard, not a rifle, bullet or cannon shot. The happy birds sang and twittered in the trees as if no war or suffering or bloodshed were near. Oh, who will undertake to describe the awful stillness and solemnity that sometimes precedes a battle? That is well understood by the experienced soldier. We passed a squad of cavalry which had gathered under a hill. As we moved on they said: "Watch out, boys." About 6 o'clock in the evening of May the 27th, the Thirty-seventh halted at the edge of an open field and laid down a few minutes. Everything was still and quiet as a Sabbath morning. In a few minutes we were ordered to charge across that field into the woods beyond it. We rushed across the field into the woods and then were in the battle of Pumpkinvine, one of the fiercest engagements of the war; and there the men of the Thirty-seventh showed their staying qualities.

As they went into the woods the enemy opened on them from their works. Our men picked up rails, old chunks and logs for breast-works and laid down behind them, and returned the enemy's fire. The battle raged furiously, and while daylight lasted, rebel sharp shooters killed and wounded many. But as I remember it, night soon came on, but the fighting continued. Our brave men seemed willing to make any sacrifice, even that of life, rather than be driven before the enemy of our country. They fired their last cartridge and then took from their dead comrades the cartridges they had in their cartridge-boxes when they fell, and fired them at the enemy. And when these were expended, no word of complaint was made as they heard the command, "When your last shot is fired, use the bayonet."

Right gladly would those brave men have obeyed the order to charge had such an order been given. As Comrade Roberts, of Co. F, says, in speaking of that battle: "If duty was shirked or responsibility transferred there, let the doubting tell, but leave to us, as comrades, the proud memories of Pickett's mill."

William Spear, of Co. F, and fourteen enlisted men of the Regiment were killed, and about sixty officers and enlisted men were wounded there that evening. I can only remember the names of a few of the killed and wounded, and therefore will not give the names of any of those true men, further than to state that Col. Ward was struck on the cheek with a minnie ball.

We held our position till late at night—till works could be constructed at the rear, and until our dead and wounded were carried back. All the dead excepting Lieut. Spear and Private Benjamin Lenover were taken back. Their bodies had been carried back part of the way, but for some cause were overlooked. A few weeks before this battle, Lieut. Spear had returned to the Regiment from an absence on a recruiting furlough, with two recruits. One of these died just after the battle of Resaca, and the other, George Godert, and the recruiting officer, Lieut. Spear, lost their lives at Pumpkinvine. Curious occurrences like this incline old soldiers to become fatalists. It is easy for them to conclude that they will not die till their time comes, and that then they will die. Hence they often become reckless. About 11 o'clock that night we were ordered back and moved across the breast-works that had been erected at the rear, and laid down near Pumpkinvine creek—"The weary to sleep and the wounded to die." Col. Ward informs me that during the fight he sent word back to Brigade headquarters three times that his Regiment was flanked, and that each time word was sent to him to hold his position and aid should be sent, but it never came. The reason no aid was sent is not creditable to the Brigade Commander, and I will say nothing about it.

Comrade Roberts says as they were going into the battle, J. J. Kirk, of Co. F, picked up a rotten looking log several inches through and about five feet in length. John Withrow, who was by his side, criticised him for such seemingly useless precaution. Kirk said to him: "You will be glad to get your head behind this log before long." When the battle line was formed and bullets were flying thick, sure enough Kirk and Withrow were lying side by side behind that chunk. As the battle raged furiously and men fell thick and fast, Kirk said: "You made fun of me for carrying this chunk, and just as I said, you are the first man to get behind it." Suddenly Kirk sprang from the line, his face covered with blood. A rebel bullet had gone through the rotten chunk and into his head, but not deep enough to prove fatal. He went to the rear, leaving his gun. In the meantime Withrow's gun got out of order, and he reached for Kirk's and fought to a finish the job they began in partnership. So that chunk saved Kirk's life, and his gun for future battles. Kirk lives in Huron, Ind., as good a citizen as he was a soldier. Withrow has long since joined that silent Company, of whom the poet says

"How sleep the brave who sink to rest
By all their country's wishes blest."

Sherman in his memoirs was unfair to us in failing to mention our battle on the 27th. Johnson mentions this battle as being one of the fiercest of the Atlanta campaign, and says that the fight which McPherson had on the 28th and of which Sherman makes favorable mention, was trifling as compared to this. No Regiment lost more men in that battle than did the Thirty-seventh Indiana and Seventy-eighth Penn. Our division Commander, Gen. Johnson, publicly congratulated us on our valor and soldierly conduct at that battle, yet Sherman does not mention the fight.

One morning two or three days after the battle, a nice-looking, old gentleman, wearing a tall plug hat and a long linen coat, came walking along the Regiment, inquiring for Co. K. That man was Chambers Stewart. His son, John M. Stewart, as good and brave a man as ever lived, belonged to Co. K, and he and Robert Thompson, of that Company, and a good and brave man, had both been killed at Pumpkinvine. Mr. Stewart came down to take the body of his son home.

At that time it was understood that no citizen could get farther south than Nashville, Tenn. An old citizen was a show down there, and his purpose seemed absurd, in view of the fact that there were strict orders against sending dead bodies home. But Mr. Stewart was there and requested me to go with him to Gen. Johnson's headquarters and get permission of him to get his son's body and take it home. I had no idea that permission would be granted, but went with him and introduced him to the General. Mr. Stewart told what he wanted and handed Gen. Johnson a letter he had gotten from Gen. Thomas. To my great surprise, Gen. Johnson, who was a gentleman, said: "Yes, Orderly, get an ambulance and take your Company or as many men as your Captain may think he may need and go and get the body."

He wrote out the order and I took it to Capt. Reeve, and he sent the Company under command of Lieut. Hunt with an ambulance and we started for that grave, a distance of three miles. We had some brisk skirmishing to get to the graves, as our army had swung around to the left and the enemy followed us. We took one prisoner during our skirmishing. We were only enabled to drive the enemy's pickets back by making them think we had a great army with us. Lieut. Hunt put our men in my command and deployed them out longer than a Regiment, and I gave commands as if I had a Battalion, while Hunt seemed to command a Brigade. When our Company first saw the enemy's pickets they commenced firing at them, which seemed to amaze Mr. Stewart. It seemed strange to him that men at the first sight of others would commence shooting at them.

We took up the body, put it in the ambulance, took it to the railroad station, and Mr. Stewart took it home. This great favor was granted to Mr. Stewart because he was a kinsman of a Mr. Beattie, a civilian who was permitted to go with the army just because Gen. Thomas liked him and had use for him at times. Mr. Stewart had reached Mr. Beattie by telegram and got him to get the favor from Gen. Thomas.

At that battle William Davis, of Co. K, was one of the color guards, and was lying down and shooting. Thomas Cox, of Co. I, was a short distance behind him. A minnie ball struck W. Davis on the side of his shoe, grazed the flesh and tore the sole off his shoe, and went back and cut a piece out of T. Cox's shoulder. Davis says his leg was paralyzed for a time and he thought he was seriously wounded. He told Cox that he was hit and Cox said he was too. Davis felt down for his wound, but found none, and his leg having become all right again, he said: "Tom, I don't believe I'm hurt."

Thomas, having examined himself in the meantime, said: "Neither am I, and here's at 'em again," and they both commenced sending bullets to the front again. I feel inclined to notice another curious thing connected with the battle of Pumpkinvine creek. After the battle, James Leeds, of Co. D, was missing. Whether he had been killed or captured could not be ascertained. A week or two after the battle some of the Thirty-seventh men picked up a scrap of paper printed in Atlanta. This paper told of the Confederate loss and the punishment the Yankees had received in that engagement, and revealed the fact that James Leeds, of the Thirty-seventh Indiana, had been wounded and captured. James died of his wounds at Atlanta.

I. E. Gary, Co. A.
Minneapolis, Minn.

After falling back on the night of the 27th, and without knowing or caring much where we were, we laid down and slept in an isolated position by a small creek till the rattle of infantry and roar of artillery aroused us from our slumbers. Fragments of shell were falling on the ground where but a few minutes before the boys slept all unconscious of war's realities. We remained there all the day inactive, but exposed to stray shot and shell and rifle balls, one of which, a minnie ball, killed a Co. I man. Another man of that Company was wounded while the Regiment lay there. All day long the firing was kept up, and about an hour before dark the conflict on our right arose to the dignity of a battle, and closely attracted our attention, as it seemed at times to be coming nearer to us and threatening to involve us in the conflict. We afterwards learned that that fight was McPherson repulsing an assault of the enemy.

The Confederate General, Joe Johnson, in his history of the Atlanta campaign, criticises Sherman for speaking of this fight in his memoirs and ignoring that of Pumpkinvine, which was of much greater magnitude. Johnson having failed to turn Sherman's right, Sherman determined to turn Johnson's right. His failure at Pickett's mill—or, rather, Pumpkinvine creek, did not cause him to abandon his purpose. He persisted in this till the 5th of June, and every effort brought on a brisk engagement.

M. I. Boully, Co. K.
Elwood, Ind.

The morning of the 29th of June we moved to the front and under cover of a hill. Our division—Gen. Johnson's, was well fortified and waiting an attack. History says Hood moved against Johnson's position, but finding it intrenched, he was recalled. At this place Gen. Johnson, of our division, issued and had read his order complimenting us for our gallant behavior at the battle of Pickett's mill.

The old mill had been burned since the battle of the 27th, and on that day, the 29th, the Thirty-seventh Indiana and the Seventy-eighth Pennsylvania let the water out of the dam and caught a few fish and turtles, all indifferent to the noise of the skirmishers and forgetful of the dangers past and yet in store for them. The morning of the 30th we again moved a few hundred yards to the left. We were close to the enemy's works, yet they were scarcely visible because of the dense woods. The country there is a succession of hills and ravines. There were scarcely any roads there, and the enemy's positions were a succession of ambushes. Of course we had to feel our way carefully. We pressed on, skirmishing and expecting a battle before night, but there was none. About this time, I do not know the exact date, the Thirty-seventh lay behind strong works, and in front of them about sixty rods the rebels were also behind good works. Our line extended far to the north and east through an open woods.

There was lively firing, but nothing more. All at once the firing on our left became very fierce, and it was evident that the firing was done by the enemy. Then we saw our line of battle break and run like arrant cowards. Our hearts almost melted within us. Soon, we supposed, the enemy would swing around and pour an enfilading fire on us, and the battle and bloodshed would be fearful. Just then we saw our soldiers returning to their places as fast as they could run. They got back to their position and soon drove back the rebel forces. Never in all my life did I love Union soldiers as I did those. They had left their guns behind and gone forward to intrench themselves, and when attacked, ran back for their guns, got them and held their position. Good, brave fellows that they were!

Our division—Johnson's, was the extreme left up to June 1st, and on that day Hooker passed to our left, and Schofield to his left. We still lay in our trenches so close to the enemy that our pickets could hear them talking. On the 1st and 2d there was a noticeable absence of artillery firing all along the line, but great activity of the Infantry. We were on the front line on the 2d and near the enemy's works. About 9 o'clock a. m., Col. Sirwell, who was in command of the Seventy-eighth Pennsylvania Regiment, crawled to our position as we lay along a hillside in a woods. He said his Regiment was in ambush at the foot of the hill below our left in a hollow and without any protection or picks or shovels. Co. F being on the extreme left of our Regiment, he asked some of the Company to volunteer to go forward to an elevated point in a field where from appearances a battery was fortified, and, if possible, get some picks and shovels.

Three men went, and they will never forget that adventure. They ran from one protecting object to another to the point for which they started, and returned the same way, rebel sharp shooters sending showers of bullets after them as they went and returned. It was a most perilous undertaking, and that not one of them was killed or seriously wounded, is nearly miraculous. They got no intrenching tools, and never heard how the Colonel and his Seventy-eighth came out of their perilous condition.

In the afternoon the rain poured down in torrents, and there was hard fighting on the left. At the close of the day we were relieved and took our position on the second line of works. The morning of June 3d opened up with vigorous skirmishing, which continued incessantly throughout the entire day and most of the night.

Shrubs, and some saplings from four to six inches in diameter, that stood in the rear of our works, were cut down by the bullets of the enemy—not cannon balls, but minnie balls. Toward evening of that day we moved to the left and took our position in the rear of our Brigade. Jeff. C. Davis' division passed in our rear and formed on our left on the 4th. That was a damp, disagreeable day, and it looked as if it might have afforded an excuse to rest, so unpleasant was it. But not so. It seemed as if the exposure to mud and water only irritated the contending armies, both of which seemed to fear the other might attempt to take some advantage offered by the unfavorable surroundings—the disagreeable weather. Consequently, there was no cessation of Infantry firing, and men were compelled to lie in the trenches, though they were muddy, and in places half full of water.

Companies A and B were detailed at night to go on picket. Companies D and F relieved them in the morning, and took their places in a light, drizzling rain. Picket firing was kept up with great activity till about 10 o'clock a. m., when quiet seemed to pervade the whole line. A forward movement disclosed the fact that Joe Johnson and his army had fallen back, and at noon we rested in his works, which for nine consecutive days and nights, had successfully resisted the power and valor of Sherman's conquering army. We rested during the balance of that day, if when bullets were whizzing over us can be called resting. That afternoon a Co. F man went over to search for the dead the Company had lost and left in the enemy's hands the night of the 27th. The place where they were laid was found, but none of the dead. The next morning we marched to the left, passing the twenty-third corps—Schofield's, and the twentieth—Hooker's, and saw some prisoners who were captured that morning by Hooker.

On the morning of the 7th we moved a short distance and went into camp. Camp rumors were uncommonly numerous and startling that day, and we threw up some splendid works in front of our Regiment. We were then near to a place called Ackworth. Johnson in his retreat gave us possession of Alatoona, and the railroad to that point was being rapidly repaired. The 8th was a comparatively quiet day for the Thirty-seventh. Nothing but picket firing in our front disturbed the quiet. We had been on that campaign then just one month, and remembered that during every day of that month we had heard the roar of shot and shells and the wicked whiz of minnie balls.

We thought we knew all of war's hardships, trials and dangers, and could anticipate everything that could befall us, but if anyone had told us that eighty more days like those of the last thirty, only more laborious and trying, were in store for us, we would have said: "No man can endure it." But those eighty days came, and most of our brave boys who escaped the minnie bullets, endured every hardship, braved every danger of that wonderful campaign and marched with banners flying into Atlanta.

We continued flanking and fighting Johnson and driving him and his army back from one line of earthworks to another till he took a strong position with his right extending across the railroad and his left on the mountain. Gen. Joe Johnson, not being able to maintain so long a line, contracted it till Kennesaw mountain became his center. On the morning of the 10th we started out, guided by the sound of the cannon, and determined to continue doing our duty, no matter how trying or dangerous it might be. We developed the enemy in the evening, and were forced to move slowly and cautiously. On the 11th we took our place on the second line and made log breast-works. In the evening we moved by the left flank. Comrade Roberts' notes says it rained the 12th, and we were ordered to stand in line of battle until the morning of the 13th, which we did with the rain soaking the earth and both armies. Nothing out of the ordinary picket firing occurred on the 14th, except our movement forward was still slow.

We went about a mile and formed a line of battle. A Co. D man was killed by a stray shot that day. We learned through the signal service that the rebel General, Polk, was killed that day. There was sharp fighting on our left the 15th, by McPherson's troops. We advanced our line on the 16th so close to those of the enemy that we could plainly see them. We pressed forward on the 17th, our skirmishers fighting desperately most of the time, capturing several prisoners—one of them seriously wounded. All along our battle line, several miles long, the rattle of rifles and the roar of cannons could be heard from morning till night. Our Brigade moved through a rain storm on the 18th, to the left of the third division (Baird's). In the afternoon we charged across a field to some timber.

While charging across this field the enemy's artillery opened on us with all its fury. Their shells burst on the ground, throwing dirt and rock on almost every man. A Co. cook was carrying two large kettles of coffee on a yoke across his neck, and a shell struck the ground and burst near him, throwing dirt in his coffee, but not hurting him, and his profanity was simply awful There Robert Stewart, a bright and lovely young man of Co. K, was killed. A piece of a shell struck him and tore out his bowels. As he sank to the ground he made the pitiful attempt to hold his bowels in his arms. He disposed of his little trinkets, bade the men that stopped with him good-bye, closed his eyes and said "Lord, Jesus, receive my spirit," and was no more. Comrade Roberts says: "This was the saddest scene in my three years' service."

We pressed on rapidly into the woods, which afforded some shelter from the enemy's artillery. At that point Albert Dunlap, of Co. A, was terribly mangled by a shell, and several others were hurt. That night we moved back on the second line. There was heavy firing all that day along the whole line. The enemy fell back again the next day—the 19th, toward Kennesaw mountain. Our skirmishers captured several prisoners, one a mere boy about 15 years of age, who belonged to the Georgia militia. He lay waiting patiently to be captured, never uttering a moan or complaint, or a single petition for favors. He commanded the respect of his captors, and was kindly dealt with by them. At midnight our Brigade was placed in reserve, where we remained till the afternoon of the 20th, and then we went to the front.

The enemy resisted our forward movement determinedly, but unsuccessfully. Every mile of the ground was fought over, and at last the enemy settled in their stronghold on the top of Kennesaw mountain an impregnable position by direct assault. From its crest they could see every move of our army, and they sent shot and shell with wonderful accuracy. One of our batteries engaged theirs the afternoon of the 21st, and made it quite lively for a time. The cannonading ceased at night, but the pickets kept it up all night. Of course it rained nearly all the time, making our duty the more disagreeable and laborious. Sherman, in a telegram to Halleck, noted the fact that the 21st of June was the nineteenth day of rain in that month. On the 22d we moved to the front works immediately in front of Little Kennesaw. There the enemy gave us a fearful shelling, but we were behind good works and the shells did us little harm.

About 6 o'clock in the evening it seemed as if every gun on both Kennesaws were trained on us. Then our batteries on our right and left, and Dilger,—"Buckskin's," battery at our front, answered every shot of the enemy. Such a noise as all these guns and their shot and shell made, I trust will never again be heard on this continent. We had good, strong earth-works and were comparatively safe by keeping close to the works. Men of the Thirty-seventh Indiana Regiment, forget what you will of the war for the preservation of the Union, but you cannot forget while life lasts to remember with pride and pleasure that 22d day of June, 1864. After dark that night we were relieved by a Brigade of Baird's division, and moved about one mile to the right. We here relieved a Brigade of Howard's corps, and laid down to sleep. Strong earth-works had been constructed here at great loss to the men who took the position. Many graves were here, with their little wooden head boards. A scalp of a soldier lay there unburied. A cannon ball had struck his head and left nothing but the scalp.

J. C. Barnard, Sergeant Co. B. Toledo, O.

This was what was called "Tater hill." It was an extremely dangerous position if a man got out of the trenches. In those trenches the Thirty-seventh lay ten long summer days and nights, exposed to the most determined and incessant artillery and musketry fire of which it is possible to conceive. During our stay there the fun-loving men of the Regiment would, when the enemy would cease their firing at us, climb upon the works as if taking a view of the enemy. In a very few moments the flames and smoke would leap from the mouth of the enemy's cannon on Kennesaw, and then down into the trench the boys would jump before the ball or shell could reach them. They had lots of fun in that way and caused the enemy to waste a great deal of ammunition. Men slept while cannonading was shaking the very earth on which they were lying. One evening just after dark, something caused the Federal and Confederate artillery to engage in a battle. All our batteries were throwing shells and exploding them at the top of Kennesaw mountain, and the guns of the enemy on that mountain answered shot for shot. Certainly no one ever saw a prettier sight than that. The fuse shells fired at us from the mountain top could be seen, describing a beautiful curve through the air, and coming at us with a fearful noise like some great ball of fire, and bursting over our heads.

Augustus E. Spencer, Co. F, died at Tullahoma, Aug. 8th, 1863.

Picket duty there was more than interesting. Pickets had to be relieved after dark, for a man would have had a poor chance of escaping death to go in front of our works in daytime. But once in the "hole in the ground" which the pickets had dug there was comparative safety. All night long the pickets kept up the firing. Nothing of any great moment occurred till the 27th, when Sherman made his foolhardy assault on Kennesaw, and lost over 3,000 men. Joe Johnson estimates the loss at not less than 6,000. All those good men were killed or wounded for nothing. Every private in that great army knew that that assault would prove a disastrous failure. That mad attempt made many a widow, and caused many mothers' hearts to ache for dear sons sacrificed to no purpose.

At our rear on "Tater hill" was an open field through which a small stream ran, and at which we got water. At the side of this open field beyond us was a woods. A battery of parrot guns was placed on this and trained on Kennesaw. A straight line from these guns to the top of Kennesaw would have struck our works. But in firing at the top of Kennesaw it was necessary, owing to the distance, to give the guns sufficient elevation to shoot several feet above us in order to hit the top of Kennesaw; and, strange to say, not one of the many shot and shell which that battery sent screaming over our heads exploded before it got to us. But who but those who heard the shot and shell shrieking a few feet above us can form any idea of the awful piercing noise they made in passing? And I confess that we all became very tired of it. The 30th was a day of comparative quiet. A good rain washed us off and made our trenches look and be something like a good hog wallow.

As the days came and went we were cramped in the trenches and exposed to the sun from 10 o'clock a. m. till night. We dare not go out of the trenches in the day time, for one would not be out thirty seconds till a minnie ball would admonish him to seek "his hole." When dark came then we would crawl out, and straighten our limbs for a few hours. After remaining in this position ten days we were relieved one dark night about 11 o'clock. Troops crept up quietly, and in whispers we gave them our places and began moving to the rear and right. About a half mile from where we started an artillery wagon lost the path in the woods through which we were passing. In order to find the path it became necessary to light some kind of a brilliant torch or lamp.

In a few seconds after lighting it, a flash was seen on the top of Kennesaw two miles away, and here came the flaming shell which burst in the woods near us. The torch kept blazing, and two more flashes from the same mountain top were seen, and two more fiery, screaming shells came and exploded right in our midst, but hurting no one. The curses and threats of our men became more dangerous to the man with the torch than the shells, and he extinguished it. That torch had to be lighted three or four times before we got out of that woods, and it never failed to draw the enemy's fire. We marched over to the right and front on the 3d of July and built strong breast-works, our skirmishers being engaged all the time.

John P. Lynch, Co. G.
Bath, Ind.

While we were thus engaged large bodies of troops were continually moving to the right. It was discovered on the morning of the 3d of July that Johnson had fallen back, and we were ordered in pursuit. We moved to the left as far as the Marietta road, leaving Big Kennesaw on our left, and marched through Marietta, a beautiful town, a few of whose inhabitants watched us from their verandas and front gates, but uttered no word, made no signs or gestures, and as far as I know, no Federal soldier said anything unkind to any citizen. It was a solemn procession. We felt sure the last laugh would after awhile be ours, but we did not want to laugh till the work was done.

The day was hot and we hurried on, to what we knew pretty well from the skirmishing we heard in our front was in store for us. The heat was so intense that many men sank down by the wayside.

Within three miles of the town we found the enemy, and the familiar sound of musket firing again greeted our ears. We bivouacked in an open field that night and listened to the firing of cannon and rifles till we went to sleep. Johnson's army was there near Ruff's Station in force, and behind intrenchments. We spent most of the 4th in this field. Two Brigades of our division were engaged fighting most of the 4th. The enemy was in strong works, prepared for them before they left Kennesaw. Here Col. Stoughton, of the Eleventh Michigan, had his leg shot away. Johnson fell back again the night of the 4th. Col. Ward tells how an old lady resident of that place described the battle there. She said:

Samuel Barbour, Co. G.
Lett's Corner, Ind.

"We'uns stopped and built a rail pile and got behind it. Then you'uns sent up a critter company and shot at we'uns, then you'uns sent up a foot company and shot at we'uns, and then you brought up the cannon wagon and throwed artillery at 'em, and you throwed one right through my ash hopper, and I wouldn't have taken two dollars for it."

On the morning of the 5th we learned that the enemy had fallen back again, and we pressed forward and found them again a few miles from the Chattahoochee river. Sharp fighting began as soon as we found them, which continued till night, the Thirty-seventh taking the front line about noon. We were at that time at the right of the railroad and about ten miles from the city of Atlanta, which was plainly visible from the tree tops. But how long it took and how many lives it cost to get possession of those ten miles!

The familiar sound of skirmishing greeted us as we awoke the morning of the 6th of July and erected breastworks. Two months have now passed, and every day of that time we have been under fire, and many of our good and brave comrades have been stricken down by the enemy's bullets. And but for the breast-works we had made, more than half our number would have been numbered among the dead and wounded. That evening a Co. G man was seriously wounded. On the morning of the 7th the Thirty-seventh went on the skirmish line with Co. F in reserve. The Thirty-eighth Indiana relieved us in the morning and we passed to the rear. The 8th was passed in comparative quiet, no general engagement appearing probable. We were in an open woods, the ground in our front receding towards the Chattahoochee river, which was two or more miles from us. The enemy's skirmishers were strongly intrenched between us and the river. A severe battle was brought on the 9th by the Twenty-first Ohio attempting to advance their line. In this fight the old and true tried Twenty-first Ohio, which from Stone river to

Henry Stone, Co. G.
Thorntown, Ind.

Atlanta shared with us the fortunes of war, suffered severely. Many of the men of the Thirty-seventh will remember one of their wounded who was carried back on a stretcher, suffering terrible agony from the remorseless tourniquet. The ball had cut the main artery of the leg, and that device was the only thing that could save him from bleeding to death.

Moving forward on the morning of the 10th we discovered that the enemy had, during the night, burned the bridge, and retreated to the south side of the river. Our skirmish line advanced, and found them in strong force and vindictive and determined as ever. From our camp we watched the opposing batteries firing at each other across the river. From this point we could clearly see the city of Atlanta, which I think was seven or eight miles distant. We lay in this camp a few days, drawing clothing on the 12th. All except the pickets passed the few days here gathering blackberries, which were plentiful. We remained in that beautiful camp eating and drinking as merrily as if no enemy was near, though the pickets were firing all the time. We all knew full well that we were liable to be called into action in an hour, but all acted on the principle, "Sufficient unto the day is the evil thereof." We received orders to move forward the evening of the 16th at 8 o'clock the next morning. On the morning of the 17th we packed our little earthly possessions, and stood waiting for orders to move, and listening to heavy cannonading at or near the river.

Jasper N. Stuart, Co. D.
Kellogg, Ia.

Ours was to obey orders and the orders to "forward march" did not come till noon. Then we marched up the river three miles, to the point selected for crossing. Here was a pontoon bridge, and amid the rattle of musketry and the heavy boom of cannons in the woods before us, we marched over the murky, turbid waters of the Chattahoochee river, and formed on the left of Davis' division.

At that point our mail came, and nearly everybody got a letter or letters. A battle was imminent, bullets were flying over and around us, but bullets and battles were not the rarity that sweet words from a far country, and loved ones at home were, and we got on the north side of tree stumps and stones, and read and re-read the messages from "home, sweet home." In a very short time our reverie was broken by the command we had heard for the thousandth time, "fall in!" We moved forward about a mile and bivouacked for the night. On the evening of the 19th we reached the north bank of Peach Tree creek, and that night crossed it with our division, the first, and made intrenchments.

Sergeant Major Marion Elston Co. K. killed in the battle of Atlanta.

CHAPTER THIRTEEN

The Battle of Atlanta and Siege of Atlanta.

The Thirty-seventh was on the skirmish line on the 19th and was sharply engaged all day. Our whole corps, the fourteenth, was on the south side of Peach Tree creek the morning of the 20th, and I think formed the right of the army. Hooker was on our left, and Howard to his left. McPherson's and Schofield's corps were northeast of Atlanta. Hood had superseded Johnson a few days before this, and determined to immortalize himself. On the morning of the 20th our army moved cautiously. Co. K had been on the skirmish line the night of the 19th and joined the Regiment on the morning of the 20th, away to the right of its skirmish line. The Thirty-seventh and our Brigade were in a pine woods, erecting works rapidly.

Corporal Isaiah L. Green, Co. C. Scipio, Ind.

About 10 o'clock we moved to the right and took our position in an open field without any protection. The heat of the sun as we lay there all day without any shade was almost unendurable. For as much as two hours a rebel cannon belched forth grape or canister shot at us. We laid close to the ground and these shot would strike the ground in our front, tear up the grass and bound on over us, but I believe no one was killed, but several were wounded. Time passed slowly while this was going on. About the middle of the afternoon Hood hurled his forces at our line of battle on our left. The roar of the battle from the first to the last was simply awful. At no other time did I hear such musketry firing as I heard there. We forgot the lone cannon at our front, and stood up and gazed intensely into the dark woods on our left where the battle raged. Indeed, the enemy at our front seemed to have been as impressed by the battle as we were, for they had quit shooting at us, and no doubt were anxiously waiting for news from the battle.

The firing at our left ceased and Hood had been defeated with great loss. Indeed, the loss was heavy on both sides. The ground where we were sloped in front upwards for two or three hundred yards, and we moved to the top of the raise and began throwing up breast-works. There we were subjected to an annoying artillery fire. Shells full of bullets were exploded above us, and these bullets and pieces of shell flew down among us. That was a beautiful evening as the sun sank beneath the western horizon, and we worked at our intrenchments and the enemy shelled us. I'll never forget the conduct of Lieut. Tevis that evening. He was dressed in a nice, clean uniform, and strutted back and forth on the crest of that hill, as if those bursting shells

George W. Hungate, Co. E.
Pleasantville, Ia.

were harmless soap bubbles. Our boys saw an officer on a white horse riding in our front about a half mile. They dropped their picks and shovels and got their guns and opened fire on him. That caused the battery to open on us with renewed vigor. Sergeant Will Rankin, of Co. K, was lying with his shoulders on his knapsack and his left wrist on the top and front of his head, holding in his right hand a Christian Instructor which he was reading. A shell exploded away above us, and a fluttering noise was heard and a ball from that shell struck Rankin's wrist, going through it into his brain. He died almost instantly, and his memory is still held in loving remembrance by every living member of Co. K, and by all in the Regiment who knew him.

Isaac N. Harrison, Co. K. Sterling, Kas.

When we started on that campaign on the 7th of May, John M. Stewart, Robert Stewart, William Rankin and myself formed a mess, and were close, staunch friends. And now on the 20th of July all were dead but me. All fell in battle, and I was with them and near them when they fell. This is so remarkable that I feel that my comrades will pardon me for relating it here. That night we put in most of the time till daylight throwing up works, and we had good ones by morning. We felt safe when close to our works next day, but it was very dangerous a few feet to the rear. Rebel sharp shooters were numerous, and evidently had good positions.

About 10 o'clock that morning, the 21st, Sergeant Major Marion Elston came along to the rear of Co. K, his old Company, and told us we could get beef at the rear and foot of the elevated ground. Just as he told us that, he turned to go to the next Company to the right, and as he turned a minnie bullet struck him at the side of the shoulder, and he fell to the ground. I and one or two others went to him. The blood could be heard spurting in the cavity of his body, and he asked: "What is that?" and on being told, he said: "Yes, that's it."

James Ruddell, Co. K, wounded at Stone river, Rushville, Ind.

An ambulance had been brought as near as it was safe to bring it, and we carried him back and put him in it. The ambulance driver having a holy terror of bullets, drove off before Marion got to say good-bye to us or we to him, and he waved his last good-bye to his comrades and Regiment by raising his foot up and down for several seconds. He lived but a short time after he was taken back. His loss was keenly felt by every man in the Regiment, and by all who knew him at his home in Milroy, in Rush county. As I remember these noble young men—their patriotism, intelligence, bravery and real worth, I am constrained to say that the noblest young men of the North wore the blue and fought the battles of the Union. Skirmishing continued all that day, and we lay behind our works in almost perfect safety, not knowing when we would be ordered to move, nor where.

In our front was a level open field nearly a half mile across. A small, crooked creek ran through that open space, and had cut its bed down some two or three feet in the earth. Our skirmishers, in great numbers, had crept into that, which in places was near the rebel skirmish line, and made it exceedingly dangerous for a Johnny to expose his head for any length of time above his works. Skirmishing in our front was lively all day, yet many of the Thirty-seventh men concluded that we would remain there another night, and about 6 o'clock in the evening they crawled out and made coffee in their quart cups. About the time the coffee got hot the men were called into line and ordered to climb over their works and move forward.

The order was promptly obeyed, but most of the men held their cups of steaming hot coffee in their hands, hoping that by some delay they might be permitted to drink it. The Thirty-eighth Indiana Regiment was on our left in this movement, and it and the Thirty-seventh were all the Regiments that were engaged in it. The line made by the two Regiments could not have been more perfect. We started across that open space at a "right shoulder shift," and moved rapidly on to the enemy. Their skirmishers, who were behind strong earth-works, did what they could to check our advance, but could not do much, for our skirmishers in the creek shot at every head that appeared above the rebel works, and we moved on as if there was no enemy

John M. Stewart, Sergeant Co. K, killed at the battle of Pumpkinvine Creek, Ga.

in our front, and our men concluding that the opportunity for drinking a good cup of coffee that evening was poor, poured it on the ground. The rebel batteries in front opened on us with shot and shell, and our batteries a quarter of a mile in our rear, sent them shot for shot.

Our line of battle never stopped or wavered for a single moment, though scores of shot and shell came and went screaming and bursting over our heads. On and on we went with the certainty of fate. We were within 100 yards of the enemy's skirmishers. They were behind very strong earth-works, and when they saw that nothing could keep us from walking over them and their works, and that continuing to fire on us would only be murder, which we would avenge when we came onto them, they stuck their guns' breech foremost over their works, and we marched on without stopping for a single moment. Men were detailed to take the prisoners to the rear, and on we went. We moved into an open woods, and the batteries in our front and rear were firing as rapidly as possible, cutting off great limbs of trees in our front and rear and over our heads. Limbs of trees and tree tops were falling nearly all the time. If one wants to feel how frail he is, he should hear a cannon ball strike a tree nearby him.

J. F. Spencer, Sergeant Co. F, wounded at Stone river, Dec. 31st, 1862, Moore's Hill, Ind.

We pressed on through the woods, exposed to the enemy's artillery and rifles, till we were near his works. It became evident that we would soon have to halt, and

CHAPTER FOURTEEN

The Siege of Atlanta.

Gen. Johnson, our division commander, was incredulous and kept his command in good shape, while Gen. Hooker said he would march his corps into the city for dinner. We met sickly-looking refugees as we went forward who said the city was evacuated.

Still we moved cautiously to the right a short distance to a road leading into the city. On this road we marched by fours, arms at will. Appearances soon changed, and we moved more cautiously, and finally halted.

E. R. Childs, Co. C.
Spokane, Wash.

About 8 o'clock we formed our line of battle facing to the front. There were no infantry or artillery firing, yet things looked suspicious to the old soldier, who had seen just such maneuvers before. We moved on cautiously during this oppressive calm, and soon a solid shot came screaming through our ranks. The enemy was strongly intrenched within three miles of the city, and we took position to the right of the railroad, and

Co. F went on picket, supporting the skirmish line, and had a good time eating blackberries and muscadine grapes. Heavy fighting was heard on the left during al the afternoon.

Hardee and Cheatham had attacked McPherson, who was killed that day. Once or twice the battle swept over toward our line, but never got to us. The Thirty-seventh intrenched itself in strong earth-works. Co. F went on the picket at night, and one of our batteries threw fuse shells over them into the enemy's lines. They, Co. F, would have enjoyed the sight more if the shells had gone farther above them. The forenoon of the 23d witnessed heavy skirmishing, and some artillery firing. A shell of the enemy struck our works in front of Co. H. The Eleventh Indiana battery shelled Atlanta in the afternoon. A good view of the city could be had from the position of the Eleventh, and its firing was very destructive to that portion of the city in the neighborhood of the round house.

James Harper, Co. A. Sharpsville, Ind.

On that day the siege of Atlanta began. The enemy was strongly intrenched. A direct assault on his works would have been madness. On the afternoon of the 24th we were informed that at a signal at 9 o'clock that night the pickets were to fire, the artillery was to open up along the whole line, bugles were to be blown, and the army in the trenches were to shout as if starting

CHAPTER FOURTEEN

The Siege of Atlanta.

Gen. Johnson, our division commander, was incredulous and kept his command in good shape, while Gen. Hooker said he would march his corps into the city for dinner. We met sickly-looking refugees as we went forward who said the city was evacuated.

Still we moved cautiously to the right a short distance to a road leading into the city. On this road we marched by fours, arms at will. Appearances soon changed, and we moved more cautiously, and finally halted.

E. R. Childs, Co. C.
Spokane, Wash.

About 8 o'clock we formed our line of battle facing to the front. There were no infantry or artillery firing, yet things looked suspicious to the old soldier, who had seen just such maneuvers before. We moved on cautiously during this oppressive calm, and soon a solid shot came screaming through our ranks. The enemy was strongly intrenched within three miles of the city, and we took position to the right of the railroad, and

Co. F went on picket, supporting the skirmish line, and had a good time eating blackberries and muscadine grapes. Heavy fighting was heard on the left during al the afternoon.

Hardee and Cheatham had attacked McPherson, who was killed that day. Once or twice the battle swept over toward our line, but never got to us. The Thirty-seventh intrenched itself in strong earth-works. Co. F went on the picket at night, and one of our batteries threw fuse shells over them into the enemy's lines. They, Co. F, would have enjoyed the sight more if the shells had gone farther above them. The forenoon of the 23d witnessed heavy skirmishing, and some artillery firing. A shell of the enemy struck our works in front of Co. H. The Eleventh Indiana battery shelled Atlanta in the afternoon. A good view of the city could be had from the position of the Eleventh, and its firing was very destructive to that portion of the city in the neighborhood of the round house.

James Harper. Co. A
Sharpsville, Ind.

On that day the siege of Atlanta began. The enemy was strongly intrenched. A direct assault on his works would have been madness. On the afternoon of the 24th we were informed that at a signal at 9 o'clock that night the pickets were to fire, the artillery was to open up along the whole line, bugles were to be blown, and the army in the trenches were to shout as if starting on a charge. At the appointed time the signal, sending up sky rockets, was given, and the program carried out, and pandemonium reigned. The enemy responded briskly, but no harm was done. I never heard what the object was, and suppose it was just to fool them. The Eleventh Indiana battery fired a shot into the city every five minutes during that whole night. The 25th and 26th were passed in skirmishing and artillery practice. The army of the Tennessee passed behind us to our right on the 27th. The army was being moved to the right and was threatening the Macon railroad. We saw many old friends in the Eighty-third Indiana, and some other Regiments. On the morning of the 28th the wagon train of the army of the Tennessee was still passing to the right. About noon that day our Brigade moved rapidly to the right to support Howard's army, which had been suddenly attacked by Lee and Stewart's corps of Hood's army. This was the battle of Ezra Church, and the last in defense of Atlanta. It ended as did the two preceding pitiful attempts to save the city. Night settled down over his defeated army, and Hood fell back into his intrenchments to await the end which he must have known was not in the distant future.

M. H. Day, Co. C.
Hayden, Ind.

In moving to the support of Howard we marched much of the way in the rear of our troops, and in plain view of the enemy's batteries, shots from which consid-

erably accelerated our movements as we marched rapidly to the sound of cannon and musketry to the right. We moved into position on the right of the Sixteenth army corps. At dark we began to build breast-works, and continued rather reluctantly till midnight, when we laid down to sleep; but the night being cold and our blankets back in our tents, we passed the night uncomfortably on the ground, wet from the recent rain. Our Brigade was relieved on the morning of the the 29th by troops from Davis' division, and we returned to our camp.

Hood had failed to accomplish anything for his cause, and his rashness had lost him many men, and the respect of his soldiers. This is clear from a conversation that took place between the pickets one day after one of the severe battles. One of our pickets called out, "Hello, Johnny, how many men have you got over there?" To which the Confederate answered, "Oh, about enough for another killing." Early on the morning of the 30th the enemy opened upon us with all their artillery it seemed. The skirmishers also were active, and all continued throughout the night. Who that was there can ever forget that awful and long continued roar, oftimes shaking the solid earth? What it was intended to accomplish I never knew.

The 31st was nice and quiet till in the afternoon, when skirmishing was begun again, and the rain commenced falling. We had had a nice time for soldiers since the 26th. There was almost constant cannonading, but that was directed by batteries at and against batteries, only an occasional shot or shell shrieking over us, rarely striking our works. The band of the Seventy-ninth Pennsylvania was quartered near us, and to the sound of musketry and cannon, and passing and exploding shells, they sent forth on the cool, calm night air sweet strains of music to cheer and comfort friend and foe alike. The siege of Atlanta began at the close of the battle of July 22d. Hood fell back into his intrenchments after the battle of Ezra Church, and remained there till Sherman's flank movement forced him to save his army from destruction.

Aug. 1st found us still in camp in rear of our division battle line, and on that day George H. Puntenney was appointed Sergeant Major. That day may be remembered from the fact that we drew the first ration of whisky we had had since the 21st of June, while in front of Kennesaw mountain. Not very many of the men in the Thirty-seventh Indiana cared much for whisky, and that may be the reason so little whisky was given it. Of course the usual roar of artillery and rattle of musketry was kept up. The absence of these would attract more attention then than their presence. The Twenty-third corps, Schofield's, had passed to the right of the army on the 23d. This change made the army of the Cumberland the left, Howard's the center and Schofield's the right. This move threatened to cut off the last line of supply of the Confederate army—the Macon railroad.

James W. Scott, Co. B.
Fairfield, Ind.

Schofield and Palmer, with the Fourteenth corps, were ordered to strike that railroad and destroy it. On the 2d of August our Regiment was appointed to the duty of train guard, and about 3 o'clock that evening we took up our march as train guard of the corps wagon train for Marietta, which point we reached a little after dark, and went into camp. We remained in Marietta the 3d and took a look at the town. Marietta was then our base of supplies, for when Johnson withdrew across the Chattahoochee he destroyed the railroad bridge, and until it was rebuilt supplies must be taken in wagon trains. Many of the citizens of Marietta, who left it while the many days' artillery firing at Kennesaw was going on, had returned to their homes, but seemed very unhappy, and who can blame them for it? In the evening our train was parked in an open field about a mile east of town. A detail picketed the camp, and we enjoyed a refreshing sleep on the ground, and listened to the booming of cannon away off at our front. Early on the morning of the 4th we started for the front, crossed the river on a pontoon bridge, and arrived at our destination about noon. That afternoon and the next day we cleared off our camp ground and pitched our tents in a beautiful grove to the right of the railroad.

Lewis L. Campbell, Co. A. Peoria, Ill.

But the sound of rifles and cannon assured us that the war was still going on. The 7th was a quiet day with us, but the old Fourteenth corps on our right was fiercely engaged, attacking and carrying the rifle pits in its front and losing in killed and wounded 500 men. On the morning of the 8th we started with a corps train for Marietta, and arrived there at 12 o'clock.

The remainder of the day we spent much as we pleased, some looking at the town and the soldiers on guard there. Many visited the sanitary and christian commission. The next morning we started back with the wagon train, and saw some large cannon going toward Atlanta. It is said that Sherman said: "I think those guns will make Atlanta of less value to them as a machine shop and depot of supplies." It soon commenced raining that morning, rained hard, and the roads became muddy and travel difficult. It was afternoon when we arrived in camp very tired. There was heavy cannonading on both flanks of the army till late at night, and the rain poured down most of the day and night and most of the next day. On the 12th we were ordered to march to Marietta, and after going about half a mile, returned to camp.

There was hard fighting on our front and right that day, but nothing was gained by our army. The bridge over the Chattahoochee had been completed, and a train load of supplies arrived on the 14th—the first in a long time, and we went and unloaded it. The opposing armies in the trenches were fighting as if they always intended to fight. The Regiment unloaded another train on the 16th. On the 17th the Regiment guarded a train to Marietta, and returned with it the next day, marching to the sound of distant cannon which sounded more fierce than common. Nothing of importance occurred till the 20th, when it became evident that a decisive movement was to be made in the immediate future.

CHAPTER FIFTEEN

A Great Flank Movement That Caused the Fall of Atlanta. Jonesboro the Objective Point.

On the 25th of August, I think, the army began a flank movement on Jonesboro, which was south of Atlanta some twenty miles. First the army was moved some distance to the rear, and then by the right flank to the west and south of the city. The Twentieth corps fell back to the north side of the Chattahoochee river and fortified. On the 20th an order was received from the war department requiring the Thirty-seventh Regiment to continue in the service until the 28th day of October, the date of our mustering at West Point, Ky., instead of the 18th day of September, the day on which we were sworn in at Lawrenceburg. The men had discussed that question many times in the last three years, but this was the first ruling on the question, and it decided it against us.

This added forty days to our three years' service, but we had been soldiers long enough to know it did no good to grumble. On the 25th of August we received marching orders. The Regiment moved with the corps train about four miles to the right, and camped for the night. The day was hot, but there was no fighting in our front. The army was then making a great flank movement on Jonesboro. Slocum had been placed permanently in command of the Twentieth corps, and occupied the intrenchments at the Chattahoochee river. All the sick, extra supplies, wagons, etc., were in his care. On the 26th the train attended by the Thirty-seventh, moved farther to the right. We moved on all night, making slow progress. A thunder-storm came up about 3 o'clock a. m. It was so dark that we could see nothing only the flashes of lightning. On the morning of the 27th we stopped just long enough to eat a hurried breakfast, and then moved on. About noon rebel cavalry threw shells into our train, creating some little alarm, but doing no harm. The cavalry were soon driven out of sight, and we marched forward. We went into camp in the evening to the right of the road, and near the park of our corps train. On the 28th we marched on to the right and front. Co. "F" was detailed to cut out a road through the woods for the train. We waited till the four corps trains moved out of our way. On the 28th the destruction of the West Point railroad was begun and completed. Many of the iron rails were heated and bent and twisted till it would be impossible to use them again. Some of the cuts were filled with a layer of dirt and then a layer of brush, and it looked like it would be difficult indeed to clean out this filling. Some rebel prisoners with us said we would be glad to leave there soon, as Hood would be after us; but we told them there was no danger, and on we marched, and the old flag still moved forward.

T. A. Jennings, Co. F.
Moore's Hill, Ind.

Hood said the fate of the city depended on their ability to defeat Sherman in this the last act in the great drama. Scene after scene from May 7th to the present hour had been presented to an anxious country, and they waited with bated breath for the curtain to rise on the last closing act of the grandest campaign in history. With Sherman it was no problem. His 106,000 effectives (using Hood's figures and words), inured to victory, against the 45,000, who from Dalton to Atlanta had continually turned their backs to the foe, but recites the oft told story, which in the end is but "hoping against hope." We remained here during the day. Our train was parked in a field and about noon our Regiment was ordered to reconnoiter in search of cavalry which were reported near us.

We went to the front a mile or so and finding no enemy, returned and remained till morning. We moved some distance the 30th, and went into camp at night. We made our beds, put down our blankets and expected to get a good night's sleep. Soon we were aroused and ordered to pack up and "fall in." In the whole category of words there are none that are so full of meaning to soldiers as those two little words, "fall in." He hears them in his sleep and day dreams. They always convey to the mind some anxiety or fear. Yet the old Thirty-seventh never in all her three years failed to respond promptly when that command was given it. About noon of the 31st our train preceded the Regiment. Owing to the bad condition of the roads, we had orders to repair it from place to place as it might need it. During our

Joseph Vandolah, Co. F, Kahoka, Mo.

march that day we passed our corps headquarters. The sound of cannon on our right that afternoon told of Hood's last stand at Atlanta. Despite the fact that Sherman was moving with five corps against his only line of communication, and with crushing weight writing the last chapter of the history of the Atlanta campaign, it seems that it never occurred to him to give up the city without a struggle and the shedding of blood. It is creditable to the Union soldiers that everywhere and on every occasion from Tunnel hill to Love Joys Station they met a foe worthy of their steel and honored progenitors. Those Southern soldiers did fight.

It seems that this flank movement had deceived Gen. Hood. He thought that Sherman had fallen back toward his base of supplies. He telegraphed that statement to the prominent men of the South, and they came to Atlanta to rejoice with him. Atlanta was in a blaze of glory. Young men and maidens danced, and old men and matrons rejoiced. It was indeed "On with the dance, let joy be unconfined." But a horseman arrives and tells them that Sherman's mighty army is marching around apparently as resistless as fate to Jonesboro, and will soon cut off all of Hood's communications with the South. Then light and joy faded from the faces of pure and lovely women and brave men, and the sound of clashing swords and coarse commands took the place of the violin and flute. Two corps were started to meet Sherman's five corps. They delayed them a little on the 31st, but only for a short time. All our force was directed to Jonesboro, and about 4 o'clock on the evening of the 1st of September, our good, old Fourteenth corps, under Gen. Davis, charged the enemy and cut him in twain, suffering severely itself and literally routing the enemy, killing and wounding great numbers of them. That night Hood blew up his magazines and abandoned Atlanta, and the campaign was ended. Two or three days after the battle I, as Sergeant Major of the Thirty-seventh, was ordered to take a lot of skulkers (those men of the army who had without permission dropped out of ranks as their comrades were going into the battle and staid in the rear till the battle was over and had been put under guard after the battle), and bury the dead of the enemy in our front.

They, the skulkers, were the toughest human beings I ever had anything to do with. In a pretty oak woods were about forty dead Confederates. There were sinks in the ground there three or four feet deep and twice that many feet long and wide. The bodies of these dead were too much decayed to be handled with the hands, and these skulkers cut forked oak limbs so as to make a hook of one fork and a hand holt of the other. They would put the hook under the chin of the dead and drag the body into the pit or sink and scrape the earth on them. These skulkers cared no more for these dead bodies than they would have cared for dead hogs.

As above stated, the campaign was over, but who will ever be able to tell the exact number of brave men who were killed while fighting from Tunnel hill to Jonesboro? On the 7th day of May, 124 days before the capture of Atlanta, bullets commenced flying past our ears, and nearly every single day of these 124 the Thirty-seventh Regiment heard the whizzing and shrieking of the enemy's shot and shell. During all these four months of continuous and hard fighting, no decisive battle had been fought. The Confederate army had been driven about 150 miles, but it was not defeated till after it made its stand at Jonesboro. There it was routed. That was a gallant army commanded by able and brave generals. If the Confederate army under Johnson and Hood in this campaign gave to history an unparalleled lesson of heroic resistance to superior numbers, that of Sherman's will live on and above it as an example of human endurance, perseverance, courage and patriotism. Thirty-seventh Indiana men shed their blood at Rocky Face ridge, swung around with Sherman's army through Snake Creek Gap, fought in the three days' fight at Resaca, crossed Ostanaula river, skirmished through Calhoun, Adairsville and beyond Etawah river, developed the enemy in his ambushed position near Dallas, where from May 25th to June 5th, the battles of New Hope Church, Pickett's mill or Pumpkinvine creek were fought, losing many men in killed and wounded, and never once failed to display the highest degree of bravery and patriotism. During all these long and trying days our grand old Regiment was in one continuous blaze of musketry and artillery fire amid the tangled undergrowth of small timber, down in deep and unexplored ravines, and up among the wild Altoona hills. On it went by the left flank through the nineteen days' rain in June; nothing daunted, brooking no defeat, it finally brought up under the enemy's guns at Kennesaw mountain, where it laid from June 21st to July 3d in the trenches exposed to the scorching rays of the sun, under a fierce and persistent artillery fire of the enemy.

D. S. Shafer, Co. G. Kokomo, Ind.

During the Atlanta campaign the army of the Cumberland alone lost 21,534 men in killed, wounded and captured. We spent a few days at Jonesboro, and saw the Confederate wounded brought into town in our army wagons. One thousand wounded Confederates must have been hauled back in those wagons. I got up on the wheels of one wagon that had ten wounded men in it. All were pale and weak. Some of them were from Texas, others from other States. Not one of them (though some were quite young men), uttered a moan or complaint. As they were unloaded from the wagon (all had to be lifted out of it), not one of them spoke of being hurt. Some of them set their jaws together a little tighter, but that was all. About the 8th of September we started back to Atlanta and went into camp near the south corporation line, now Peach Tree street, passing strong fortifications near the city. The city was badly torn with shot and shell from our batteries.

W. A. Bodine. Co. I.
Morristown, Ind.

Many of our men visited a fort near the city where five large sixty-four pounds cannon had been spiked when abandoned by the enemy. They were old United States pieces which had been stolen from our government by Floyd. Nothing of great importance happened the 10th, 11th, 12th and 13th, except that Gen. Sherman issued an order requiring citizens of Atlanta to go either North or South. During these days citizens— men, women and children, some of the ladies elegantly dressed and evidently unaccustomed to hardships, passed our camp on their way South. They said nothing to us and we said nothing to them. The city was literally torn to pieces; more than half the houses had been struck by one or more shots or shells. Every door yard had an artificial cave in it, into which the family went when the artillery was playing on the city. Some of us went to church one day, and it had been punctured three or four times by cannon balls.

As the Regiment had been mustered into the service on the 18th of September, 1861, it was ordered on that day in 1864 to report at Indianapolis as early as possible. On the evening of the 18th we left the camp, bidding good-bye to the good, brave boys of Companies A, B, C, D, I and K, who had shared with us in the toils, privations and dangers of many battles in which we had been engaged. We were going to home and friends and civil life, they to the honor and glory awaiting them in their march to, and camp by the sea.

Our train, a freight, composed of stock cars and platform cars, got off the 19th about 10 o'clock a. m., but we went slowly. The men were on top of the cars, in them and on the platform cars. Most of the distance to Chattanooga was made after night, and those on the platform cars and on top of the cars, in order to keep from falling off the cars when asleep, had to tie themselves to something on the car. Not much sleeping was done, but the train thundered along and got into Chattanooga about 9 o'clock of the morning of the 20th. Here we met several of the Regiment who were awaiting our arrival. At about 11 o'clock a. m. we bid farewell to Chattanooga, the scenes of many hardships and trials, and after a tiresome ride over a devastated country, arrived at Nashville. We staid there one night and part of two days, when we left and came on to Louisville.

Col. Ward without delay applied for transportation to Indianapolis, and got an order for it over the road to Jeffersonville. As the Regiment marched through Louisville to the river, it marched two abreast by platoons at times and by Companies at times. All did their level best (and but few Regiments could march or drill with the Thirty-seventh), and as the men passed on with their sunburnt hands and faces, worn garments, military step and bright guns at a "right shoulder shift" they attracted much attention. All knew we had served our full three years, and one enthusiastic bystander remarked: "That old Regiment could make a h—l of a racket yet." We crossed the river into Jeffersonville that evening. Our Colonel had some difficulty in securing a train for us, but finally succeeded after threatening to press one into the service.

We left on the 22d on an old, rickety train with a wheezy engine that made slow time indeed. The old engine gave out about the middle of the afternoon and came to a dead stand still near Vienna. We laid there till late at night waiting for another engine. It came at last, and we went on slowly, arriving at Indianapolis about 2 o'clock p. m. It was the Sabbath, and we marched into Camp Morton, got a good dinner and prepared to rest. We had not been many days in camp till Gov. Morton sent word to the Regiment that there was likely to be trouble with the Knights of the Golden Circle in Sullivan county, and he wished a trained and tried Regiment to deal with them if trouble came. He requested the Regiment to consent to remain in the service for a time, or until the danger was past.

To this request the men cheerfully consented, and remained till Oct. 27th, in the meantime receiving a furlough home to see our friends and vote at the election. All returned and were paid off and mustered out on the 27th of October, and returned to their homes and the trials and pleasures of civil life.

Our work as soldiers was done, and I think well done. The joys and sorrows of those three terrible years were in the past, but not forgotten, nor never can be by any of us while life lasts. The memories of this long companionship will be like a day dream growing brighter and more precious, as the evening of life comes on with the infirmities of age.

As I look back through the thirty-four years past at the thousand strong, young men and patriots of which the Thirty-seventh Indiana Regiment was composed—like the host of Israel which came out of Egypt, "not one feeble one among them," I am forced to conclude that the King of Nations raised them up, and others like them, for the express purpose of preserving this government, with its institutions to bless not only the people of this nation, but those of every nation on the face of the earth. Comrades, it was a glorious cause for which you fought, and glorious were your achievements. No matter how difficult or dangerous was the duty assigned you, you did it promptly and well.

Thomas A. Shirk, Co. H. Waynesburgh, Ind. Past Commander Post 134, Sardenia, Ind. One of four brothers who enlisted in 1861, and the only one to return. Two killed, and the other died in prison.

Search the history of the Regiment from the time you crossed the Ohio river into Kentucky, till you, three years afterwards, re-crossed it into Indiana to be mustered out, and the most searching critic will find no stain on it, but will find it always equal to the best of all the brave and loyal Regiments sent out by any State for the preservation of the Union. You never shirked a duty or disobeyed an order. I have no way of arriving at the exact loss of the Regiment from death and wounds,

I learn from Terrell's reports, which do not give the names of all who were wounded or killed in battle, that 170 of the Regiment either died or were killed in battle; also that 185 were disabled by disease and wounds.

That makes in all 355 men—over the third of the Regiment. But the number is much larger than that. The wounded who were not permanently disabled are not mentioned in Terrell's reports. The wounds that our Colonel, W. D. Ward, received, are not mentioned, and of course those of privates would not be. Many men were seriously wounded more than once, yet no mention is made of it. I say this to show that not half the wounds received by men of the Thirty-seventh Regiment, or any other Regiment, are given in that report. It is safe to say that more than half the men in the Thirty-seventh Regiment were killed or seriously wounded. Col. Ward says: "My old Company 'A' was composed of strong, young men, the flower of Ripley county, Indiana—101 strong. Before their time of service expired thirty-four of them were in their graves." Yet Terrell's report only names twenty-four as having been killed in battle, or died of disease. But after all, if our Regiment did not suffer enough it was because it did not have the opportunity. It was actively engaged in thirteen hard fought battles, including Stone river, Chickamauga, Resaca, Pumpkinvine creek and twice at Rocky Face ridge and Buzzard Roost, and conducted itself heroically in every one of them.

John A. Cowan, Co. K. Richland, Ind.

And now, comrades, in closing permit me to say that I know that you have comrades who could in writing this history have done you and your grand old Regiment more nearly justice than I have done, but I have done the best I could. I am greatly indebted to our comrades, Col. W. D. Ward and Leroy Roberts for the copious and elegantly written facts which they furnished me. In conclusion I will say I know that the three score and ten years allotted to man will soon be reached by most of you, and that the remaining years which may be given you, will, by reason of the hardships of war, the wounds received in battle and the increase of years be years of "labor and sorrow."

Yet, if the dates which I have given you in this attempted history, and the facts which I have so tamely, and sometimes inelegantly expressed, shall in recalling to your minds any of the sad or happy incidents of these three long years of your youth, valor and patriotism, be a source of any pleasure or profit to you, as you go on to join your comrades who have answered the roll call on the "other shore," I shall be abundantly compensated for all the time and labor the writing of this unpretentious little volume has cost me.

In conclusion, comrades, let us now and in the future, as in the day when our Regimental line melted before the fiery breath of battle, take a look at our flag, the bonniest flag the sunlight of heaven ever kissed, and close up our thinning ranks by dressing to the center till the last old patriot of the Thirty-seventh Indiana has been called from time to eternity.

CAPTAIN HEZEKIAH SHOOK, Co. D,
Versailles, Ind.

HISTORY OF CAPT. SHORT.

Capt. Charles C. Short, Co. A.
Lawrenceburg, Ind.

Capt. Charles C. Short enlisted in Co. A, Thirty-seventh Indiana Infantry, Aug. 20th, 1861, and went into camp at Lawrenceburg, Ind.; left the State as Commissary Sergeant; afterward commissioned Regimental Quartermaster. The 26th day of April, 1862, he was commissioned Second Lieutenant in the Thirty-seventh Regiment, Co. A. The 22d day of February, 1863, he was commissioned First Lieutenant in same Regiment. The 9th day of December, 1863, he was commissioned Captain. He was born June 16th, 1834; died Sept. 21st, 1881.

AN INCIDENT.

"Hold the Fort for I am Coming"—A Thirty-seventh Man Did It.

The occasion which gave rise to that once famous hymn is believed to be as follows: Lieut. J. H. Connelly, of Co. I, Thirty-seventh Indiana, whose portrait is on page 87, was transferred to the signal service. His widow copies and sends me the following notes written by her husband while on duty in the army: "Hood moved from his position south of Atlanta, and placed his army between Sherman's army and their supplies at Chattanooga. The enemy had destroyed the Western and Atlantic railroad as far as Allatoona. At 9 o'clock a. m., Oct. 5th, 1864, Gen. French's division, having made the destruction of the railroad complete to that place, attacked Allatoona, and after a furious fight of five hours, was driven away severely punished. During the day of the fight we had as visitors to Kennesaw mountain, Gen. Sherman and five other general officers of less note." Lieut. Connelly's station was on Kennesaw. The following is the message which is supposed to have given rise to the song, "Hold the fort," and which was signaled by Lieut. Connelly to Allatoona:

"Oct. 5th, '64. From headquarters. Tell Allatoona hold on. Gen. Sherman says he is working hard for you. W. T. SHERMAN, Maj. Gen."

From this was put in verse the song, "Hold the fort." Among the papers of her deceased husband, Mrs. Connelly found the following letter from Gen. Sherman to Secretary of War Staunton. The following is from the copy she sends:

He said "When the enemy had cut our lines and actually made a lodgement on our railroad about Big Shanty, the signal officers on Vinning's hill, Kennesaw and Allatoona, sent my orders to Gen. Corse at Rome, whereby Gen. Corse was enabled to reach Allatoona just in time to defend it. Had it not been for the service of this corps on that occasion, I am satisfied we should have lost the garrison at Allatoona, and a most valuable depository of provisions there which were worth to me and the country more than the aggregate expense of the whole signal corps for one year."

James H. Connelly was brevetted First Lieutenant for gallant conduct at the battle of Allatoona. That was signed by Andrew Johnson.

ROSTER THIRTY-SEVENTH INDIANA INFANTRY.

Great effort has been made to make this roster correct. The Adjutant-General's report has been relied on to a great extent, but that has been corrected in several things by the aid of comrades. No doubt there are mistakes in it, but all the men now living could not make it absolutely correct.

OFFICERS OF THE THIRTY-SEVENTH INDIANA REGIMENT.

Name and Rank	Date of Commission	Remarks
Colonel—		
George W. Hazzard	Sept. 12, 1861	Returned to regular army Mar. 5, '62
Carter Gazlay	Aug. 8, 1862	Dismissed service Aug. 13, '62
James S. Hull	Aug. 11, 1862	Mustered out with Regiment
Lieutenant-Colonel—		
Carter Gazlay	Sept. 20, 1861	Promoted Colonel
James S. Hull	April 26, 1862	Promoted Colonel
William D. Ward	Aug. 14, 1862	Mustered out with Regiment
Major—		
James S. Hull	Sept. 20, 1861	Promoted Lieutenant-Colonel
William D. Ward	April 26, 1862	Promoted Lieutenant-Colonel
Thomas V. Kimble	Aug. 14, 1862	Mustered out with Regiment
Adjutant—		
Livingston Howland	Oct. 2, 1861	Discharged August, '64
William B. Harvey	Feb. 27, 1863	Mustered out with Regiment

Quarter-master—
    Francis Riddle   Sept. 20, 1861   Resigned Aug. 7, '63
    Daniel M. Redlon   Mustered out with Regiment
Chaplain—
    John H. Lozier   Oct. 1, 1861   Mustered out with Regiment
Surgeon—
    William Anderson   Oct. 17, 1861   Mustered out with Regiment
Assistant Surgeon—
    John R. Goodwin   Sept. 22, 1861   Mustered out with Regiment
    Samuel M. McClure   Nov. 18, 1862   Resigned February, '64
Captain Co. A—
    William D. Ward   Sept. 10, 1861   Promoted Major
    William Hyatt   April 26, 1862
    Charles C. Short   Dec. 6, 1863   Resigned Dec. 5, '63
First Lieutenant—
    William Hyatt   Sept. 10, 1861   Promoted Captain
    Washington Stockwell   April 26, 1862   Dismissed February, '63
    Charles C. Short   Feb. 22, 1863   Resigned Aug. 13, '64
    John Sage   Dec. 6, 1863   Mustered out with Regiment
    Thomas Kirk   Aug. 14, 1864   Transferred to Co. B residuary Battalion
    James Coulter   Dec. 24, 1864   Mustered out with Battalion
Second Lieutenant—
    Washington Stockwell   Sept. 10, 1861   Promoted First Lieutenant
    Charles C. Short   April 26, 1862   Promoted First Lieutenant
    John Sage   Feb. 22, 1863   Promoted First Lieutenant

Name and Rank	Date of Commission	Remarks
B Captain—		
Thomas V. Kimble	Sept. 10, 1861	Promoted Major
Robert M. Goodwin	Aug. 14, 1862	Resigned to accept promotion
First Lieutenant—		
Robert M. Goodwin	Sept. 10, 1861	Promoted Captain
William H. Wilkinson	Aug. 14, 1862	Mustered out with Regiment
Second Lieutenant—		
William H. Wilkinson	Sept. 10, 1861	Promoted First Lieutenant
Jacob W. Stoner	Aug. 14, 1862	Mustered out with Regiment
C Captain—		
Thomas W. Pate	Sept. 10, 1861	Cashiered Dec. 26, '63
Robert C. Pate	April 19, 1863	Mustered out with Regiment
First Lieutenant—		
James T. Matteson	Sept. 10, 1861	Resigned Dec. 25, '63
Robert C. Pate	Dec. 26, 1862	Promoted Captain
John S. Henry	April 19, 1862	Mustered out Sept. 22, '64
Second Lieutenant—		
Robert C. Pate	Sept. 10, 1861	Promoted First Lieutenant
John S. Henry	Dec. 26, 1862	Promoted First Lieutenant
James M. Hodshire	April 19, 1863	Revoked
Socrates Carver	April 19, 1863	Promoted Captain
D Captain—		
Hezekiah Shook	Sept. 10, 1861	Mustered out with Regiment
First Lieutenant—		
Jesse B. Holman	Sept. 10, 1861	Killed at Stone River, Dec. 31, '62

William H. Pye	Jan. 1, 1863	Resigned Feb. 22, '64
Second Lieutenant—		
James M. Hartley	Sept. 10, 1861	Died of disease
William H. Pye	May 30, 1862	Promoted First Lieutenant
George W. Cowan	Jan. 1, 1863	Mustered out with Regiment
E Captain—		
Mahlon C. Connett	Sept. 10, 1861	Resigned Feb. 26, '63
Frank Hughes	Feb. 27, 1863	Died from wounds July 28, '64
William B. Harvey	Aug. 7, 1864	Mustered out with Regiment
First Lieutenant—		
Frank Hughes	Sept. 10, 1861	Promoted Captain
William B. Harvey	Feb. 27, 1863	Assigned as Adjutant
George W. Hungate	Aug. 7, 1864	Mustered out with Regiment
Second Lieutenant—		
Andrew J. Hungate	Sept. 10, 1861	Resigned Nov. 21, '62
William B. Harvey	Nov. 22, 1862	Promoted First Lieutenant
George W. Hungate	Feb. 27, 1863	Mustered out with Regiment
F Captain—		
Wesley G. Markland	Sept. 10, 1861	Mustered out with Regiment
First Lieutenant—		
John B. Hodges	Sept. 10, 1861	Mustered out with Regiment
Second Lieutenant—		
Joseph P. Stoops	Sept. 10, 1861	Resigned Dec. 11, '62
William Spears	Dec. 12, 1862	Killed at battle Pumpkinvine, May 27, '64
G Captain—		
John McCoy	Sept. 10, 1861	Resigned Nov. 21, 1861

Name and Rank	Date of Commission	Remarks
Henry E. Lord	Nov. 24, 1861	Resigned March 22, '64
Daniel S. Shafer	March 23, 1864	Mustered out with Regiment
First Lieutenant—		
Archibald F. Allen	Sept. 10, 1861	Resigned Dec. 11, '62
Daniel S. Shafer	Dec. 12, 1862	Promoted Captain
William H. Baughman	March 23, 1864	Promoted to First Lieutenant
Second Lieutenant—		
Daniel S. Shafer	Sept. 10, 1861	Promoted First Lieutenant
William H. Baughman	Dec. 12, 1862	Promoted First Lieutenant
H Captain		
William H. Tyner	Sept. 10, 1861	Discharged March 6, '62
Quartus C. Moore	March 15, '62	Discharged for disability Dec. 9, '62
George W. Pye	Dec. 10, 1862	Resigned Feb. 2, '63
James H. Burke	Feb. 3, 1863	Died from wounds July 9, '64
John L. Hice	July 10, 1864	Mustered out with Regiment
First Lieutenant—		
Quartus C. Moore	Sept. 10, 1861	Promoted Captain
George W. Pye	March 15, 1862	Promoted Captain
James H. Burke	Dec. 10, 1862	Promoted Captain
John L. Hice	Feb. 3, 1863	Mustered out with Regiment
Augustus H. Tevis	July 10, 1864	Mustered out with Regiment
Second Lieutenant—		
George W. Pye	Sept. 10, 1861	Promoted First Lieutenant
James H. Burke	March 15, 1862	Promoted First Lieutenant
John L. Hice	Dec. 10, 1862	Promoted First Lieutenant

INDIANA VOLUNTEER INFANTRY. 145

Augustus H. Tevis—	Feb. 3, 1863	Promoted First Lieutenant
I Captain—		
William N. Doughty	Sept. 10, 1861	Mustered out with Regiment
First Lieutenant—		
John Bleakey	Sept. 10, 1861	Resigned June 6, '64
James H. Connelly	June 7, 1862	Transferred to signal corps
Second Lieutenant—		
Isaac Abernathy	Sept. 10, 1861	Promoted First Lieutenant Co. K
James H. Connelly	Nov. 24, 1861	Promoted First Lieutenant
George W. Meyer	June 7, 1863	Promoted Captain
K Captain—		
John McKee	Sept. 10, 1861	Wounded at Stone river—Discharged
John B. Reeve	Oct. 22, 1862	Mustered out with Regiment
First Lieutenant—		
Henry E. Lord	Sept. 10, 1861	Promoted Captain Co. G
Isaac Abernathy	Nov. 24, 1861	Killed at Stone river
John B. Reeve	Jan. 1, 1863	Promoted Captain
William R. Hunt	Oct. 29, 1863	Mustered out with Regiment
Second Lieutenant—		
John B. Reeve	Sept. 10, 1861	Promoted First Lieutenant
John Patton	Jan. 1, 1863	Died from wounds rec'd at Stone river
William R. Hunt	Feb. 22, 1863	Promoted First Lieutenant

THIRTY-SEVENTH REGIMENT INFANTRY STAFF AND BAND.

Sergeant Major—
  Connelly, James H., promoted to Second Lieutenant Co. I.
Commissary Sergeant—
  Short, Charles C., promoted to Second Lieutenant Co. A.
Hospital Stewart—
  Lupton, George, discharged Dec. 28, '61.
Principal Musicians—
  Gorsuch, Joseph B., mustered out March 16, '62; Nowotney, John L., mustered out May 3, '62; band mustered out early in '62; Hunter, Alfred G.; Ellis, Edwin; Lawless, P. J.; Watkins, Green S.; Bennie, John; Pullman, William W.; Price, Joel B.; Brison, Hugh; Mix, S. M.; Shellenberger, William D.; Hope, John S.; Passel, George W.; Bardwell, Milner; Evans, James; Glasgow, W. R.; Hamlin, Omer; Huids, Francis M.; Jenning, William W.; Johnson, Benjamin F.; Murphy, James S.; Picket, Ira B.; Schofield, Eden C.; Soper, Melville H.; Stewart, W. K.

Enlisted Men of Co. A.

First Sergeant—
  Sage, John, promoted to Second Lieutenant.
Sergeants—
  Elrod, William D., mustered out Oct. 27, '64.
  Kirk, Thomas, veteran, promoted to First Lieutenant.
  Firth, Luke, veteran.
  Brown, John.
Corporals—
  Grossman, John, died of wounds received in action.
  Lane, Henry, mustered out Oct. 27, '64.
  Stockwell, John, veteran.

Powell, James M.
Smitha A. W.
Pendergast, William P., mustered out Oct. 27, '64.
Louis, William H., died of wounds received in action.
Casteter, Ira, veteran.

Musicians—
Jemison, Elias, mustered out Oct. 27, '64.
Campbell, Lewis, mustered out Oct. 27, '64.

Wagoner—
Titus, John.

Privates—
Albright, Joseph, mustered out Oct. 27, '64.
Alfrey, Henry, mustered out Oct. 27, '64.
Austin, John, died Feb. 25, '62.
Austin, Wesley, died at Elizabethtown, Ky., Dec. 6, '61.
Bailey, Wilson, veteran.
Bebee, James, killed at Stone river.
Benham, John, mustered out Oct. 27, '64.
Benham, Shedrack, died at Elizabethtown, Ky., Jan. 4, '62.
Bruner, Oliver, died of wounds received in action.
Buckhannan, George.
Buckhannan, John.
Caplinger, Jacob M., veteran.
Cole, William, veteran.
Copeland, Smith W.
Craven, Thomas.
Craven, Wesley, veteran.
Curran, James.
Curran, Newton, veteran.
Custer, Jethro, died at Bacon creek, Kentucky, Jan. 31, '62.
Dunlap, Albert G., killed in action.
Durman, James, discharged Jan. 20, '63.
Ent, Asher, died at Elizabethtown, Ky., Dec. 10, '61.

French, Peter.
French, John.
Gary, Imlac E., mustered out Oct. 27, '64.
Gookins, Harrison, veteran, died at Savannah, Ga., Jan. 10, '65.
Grecian, Isaac, veteran Co. A.
Hannars, John, veteran.
Harmon, David, mustered out Oct. 27, '64.
Harper, James, mustered out Oct. 27, '64.
Hasting, James, died at Elizabethtown, Ky., December, '61.
Hasty, John, mustered out Oct. 27, '64.
Harvey, James, mustered out Oct. 27, '64.
Heller, John, killed in action.
Herndon, Benjamin, mustered out Oct. 27, '64.
Hess, Theodore, veteran.
Hicks, John W., died of wounds received in action.
Hyatt, Shedrack, discharged Dec. 12, '61, disability.
Jackson, Lemuel, killed in action.
Jackson, Rufus.
Johnson, Erastus, died March 15, '62.
Kelly, Charles F., died Feb. 20, '62.
Kelly, Daniel, killed in railroad accident.
Kelly, Lafayette, died at Grayville, Ga., April 11, '64.
Kelly, Silas.
Kelly, William, veteran.
Kirk, John W., mustered out Oct. 27, '64.
Laswell, John.
Laswell, Thomas.
Main, Josephus.
Mathey, Charles, died at Chattanooga, Tenn., Dec. 5, '63.
May, Samuel S., mustered out Oct. 27, '64.
McCasky, John H., discharged Dec. 5, '62.
McCasky, William F.
McKitrick, Ludlow, died of wounds received in

action.
Moncrief, John B., discharged March 12, '63.
Moreland, Jesse G., died of wounds received in action.
Morrow, James, died at Elizabethtown, Ky., Dec. 5, '61.
Myers, James C., veteran.
Myers, George A., died of wounds received in action.
Northern, James H., discharged Feb. 9, '63.
Osborn, Joseph C.
Papet, Samuel, died at Louisville, Jan. 15, '62.
Pardum, Leander, died June 5, '62.
Parsons, William, transferred to signal corps Oct. 22, '63.
Payton, John C., veteran.
Pendergast, Hiram, mustered out Oct. 27, '64.
Ross, William L., killed in action.
Shook, Abraham, discharged, disability, July 24, '62.
Smith, Orsam, mustered out Oct. 27, '64.
Spears, Joseph J., veteranized.
Stage, Theodore, died at Elizabethtown, Ky., Dec. 18, '61.
Sutton, Reuben, veteran.
Swing, Jeremiah, veteranized.
Titus, Harvey, died Oct. 21, '62, accidental wounds.
Vayhinger, Edwin, died at Elizabethtown, Ky., Dec. 8, '61.
Waylan, William A., veteranized.
Westover, William, mustered out Oct. 27, '64.
Williamson, Stephen, died at Murfreesboro, Feb. 3, '63.
Wright, George, veteranized.
Wright, James.
Young, Amaziah.
Recruits—
Ward, Jonathan B., mustered out Dec. 16, '64.

Craven, John.
Allen, William.
Delap, Nathaniel.
Mavity, Samuel.

Enlisted Men of Co. B.

First Sergeant—
  Morflitt, Charles W., discharged May 29, '62, disability.
Sergeants—
  Stoner, Jacob W., promoted to Second Lieutenant.
  Colter, James, veteranized.
  Price, John S., discharged, disability.
  Davis, Marion, veteranized.
Corporals—
  Goudie, J. A. H., discharged, disability, March 21, '63.
  Davison, John A., mustered out Oct. 27, '64.
  Barnard, James C., veteranized.
  Winnins, William F., veteranized.
  Ailes, Fletcher W., mustered out Oct. 27, '64.
  Wiley, Spencer, mustered out Oct. 27, '64.
  Graw, George C., mustered out Oct. 27, '64.
  Brown, James E., transferred V. R. C.
Musicians—
  Barlow, William H. H.
  Marquet, Jacob, veteranized.
Wagoner—
  Sherman, A., I , mustered out Oct. 27, '64.
Privates—
  Anderson, Lucius L., veteranized.
  Alford, William, mustered out Oct. 27, '64.
  Bassett, William J., transferred V. R. C.
  Bassett, Charles H., discharged, loss of speech, July 15, '62.
  Baker, Joshua, veteranized.
  Barnard, Oliver W., veteranized.

Bartlow, James H., veteranized.
Bell, Selby, discharged Aug. 24, '63.
Bell, Andrew M., veteranized.
Bloom, George, veteranized.
Bloom, William P.
Bowers, Myer, veteranized.
Bowen, Thomas J., veteranized.
Britton, Alfred D., discharged, disability, Jan. 14, '63.
Burrus, George K., mustered out Oct. 27, '64.
Burns, Matthew B., died.
Case, Barion L., transferred Sig. C., Oct. 22, '63.
Clark, Henry D., mustered out Oct. 27, '64.
Cuchsondoffer, John, discharged Nov. 26, '62.
Curtis, Levi S., discharged, disability, Feb. 4, '62.
Davison, Lewis A., mustered out Oct. 27, '64.
Egbert, Josiah, died Dec. 31, '62, of wounds.
Fisk, William, died of wounds.
Forrow, Martin H., veteranized.
Foster, Ellis W., veteranized.
Freeman, John P.
Gard, Daniel H., died at Nashville, Tenn., April 19, '62.
Guyer, John H., veteranized.
George, James D., discharged, disability, July 2, '63.
Graper, William F., veteranized.
Grob, Michael, veteranized.
Green, James A., veteranized.
Harvey, William W., veteranized.
Hern, William F.
Higdon, Eli W., diischarged, disability, Nov 26, '62.
Hollingsworth, Joseph, veteranized.
Hollingsworth, Joel, died at Elizabethtown, Ky., Dec. 17, '61.
Hoffman, John, mustered out Oct. 27, '64.
Hoffman, George, died at Bear Creek Dec. 30, '61.
Kempker, William L., veteranized.

Kelly, Reuben, died.
Kruse, Frederick, mustered out Oct. 27, '64.
Lewis, Nathan, mustered out Oct. 27, '64.
Lynn, James H., discharged, disability, Dec. 26, '62.
Maple, John M., discharged, disability, May 9, '62.
Magoon, Josiah, transferred Sig. C., Oct. 22, '63.
Miller, Herman, died.
Mitchell, Daniel, discharged, disability, '62.
Moor, Brice B.
Morgan, James M., discharged Nov. 27, '62.
Morrow, James, discharged Feb. 27, '62, disability.
Morgan, Samuel, discharged Feb. 27, '62, disability.
Miller, Samuel Y., mustered out Oct. 27, '64.
Montgomery, Samuel, discharged Aug. 11, '62, disability.
McCon, John, discharged Nov. 28, '62.
McCrady, John, died at Murfreesboro, Tenn.
McCullum, Edward, veteranized.
McKnight, William J., mustered out Oct. 27, '64.
Nutt, Levi, veteranized.
Phillips, Eli, veteranized.
Roberts, Francis M., mustered out Oct. 27, '64.
Rodgers, George W., killed at Stone river Dec. 31, '62.
Rose, Allen C., discharged July 11, '63, disability.
Rodgers, William P., mustered out Oct. 27, '64.
Rolf, Walter C., mustered out Oct. 27, '64.
Skinner, William H., transferred V. R. C. '63.
Smalley, Elbert M., mustered out Oct. 27, '64.
Smith, James, veteranized.
Scudder, R. M.
Snyder, Isaac N., killed at Stone river Dec. 31, '62.
Stewart, James M., mustered out Oct. 27, '64.
Thompson, Samuel, veteranized.
Vanmeter, Thomas G., veteranized.
Williams, James, discharged Oct. 9, '62, disability.

Weidner, William, veteran.
Wolstonholm, John, veteranized.
Winans, Frazer N., veteranized.
Wilkinson, Isaac, veteranized.
Walker, Hiram L. A., discharged Feb. 7, '62, disability.
Weston, Hiram J., mustered out Oct. 27, '64.
Yates, Joseph, mustered out Oct. 27, '64.
Young, Sandford, died at Andersonville, Ind., Feb. 25, '62.

Enlisted Men of Co. C.

First Sergeant—
  Ewan, James S.
Sergeants—
  Henry, John S., promoted Second Lieutenant.
  McKinney, Samuel, mustered out Oct. 27, '64.
  Carver, Socrates, promoted Second Lieutenant.
  Hodshire, James M., mustered out Oct. 27, '64.
Corporals—
  Wheeler, Levi E.
  Buck, Peter.
  Day, Mitchell H., veteranized.
  Carney, Joseph W.
  Doyle, William, mustered out Oct. 27, '64.
  Grinstead, Henry P.
  Kelly, Robert J., mustered out Oct. 27, '64.
  Green, Isaiah, mustered out Oct. 27, '64.
Musicians—
  Rogers, A.
  Reser, William.
Wagoner—
  Rockey, Nathan.
Privates—
  Baker, Stephen, veteranized.
  Blanchard, Chapman.

Caray, Patrick, discharged Dec. 30, '62, disability.
Child, Edwin R., veteranized.
Chamberlain, Francis W., veteranized.
Cole, James W., discharged Aug. 6, '62, disability.
Cole, William J., discharged April 21, '62, disability.
Cooper, Eli, died at Huntsville, Ala., Sept. 6, '62.
Curtis, N. H., discharged March 5, '62.
Davis, Robert, discharged April 21, '63, disability.
Davidson, Robert, mustered out Oct. 27, '64.
Edwards, Robert H., veteranized.
Emmert, William, veteranized.
Emmert, Jacob.
Ferren, James A. C.
Ferren, John H., died at Bacon creek, Ky., Dec. 29, '61.
Fisk, Brower.
Force, Benjamin, veteranized.
Force, Nelson K., veteranized.
Fowler, William, mustered out Oct. 27, '64.
Goltry, Jacob F., veteranized.
Goltry, David, veteranized.
Gorbert, John, mustered out Oct. 27, '64.
Gordon, Thomas, mustered out Oct. 27, '64.
Gordon, Richard S., discharged Feb. 19, '63.
Grinstead, Henry P., died at Bacon creek, Kentucky, Jan. 5, '62.
Hammond, William, discharged Feb. 4, '62, disability.
Hankins, Joshua, mustered out Oct. 27, '64.
Hirsh, Jacob, discharged Nov. 26, '62.
Henson, John, mustered out Oct. 27, '64.
Jackson, O. P.
Johnson, William F., veteranized.
Justis, Lewis.
Kinnet, Wiley, veteranized.
Kinnet, James, mustered out Oct. 27, '64.
Kinnet, Abraham, veteranized.

Land. Samuel, discharged Jan. 23, '63.
Lackner, Joseph, died at Elizabethtown, Ky., Dec. 14, '61.
Lawler, John.
Long, Woodson, veteranized.
Liggett, Edwin, mustered out Oct. 27, '64.
Myer, Henry, discharged Jan. 14, '63.
McGuire, Michael, mustered out Oct. 27, '64.
McKay, George.
McLain, Robert, veteranized.
McLain, Tilford, veteranized.
Minor, Joseph, veteranized.
Meek, James H., veteranized.
Moore, George, discharged Feb. 3, '64, disability.
Morgan, Isaac N., veteranized.
Moulton, Christopher.
Morton, John, veteran.
Myers, William V., discharged June 19, '62, disability.
Jackson, O. P.
Pate, James.
Pate, Benjamin F., mustered out Oct. 27, '64.
Phillips, William, veteranized.
Powell, Joseph, veteran.
Prebel, John F., died at Bacon creek, Kentucky, Jan. 5, '62.
Prebel, Jesse A., mustered out Oct. 27, '64.
Reser, Lewis, died at Chattanooga Oct. 26, '63.
Rice, Cyrus, died at Bacon creek, Kentucky, Dec. 25, '61.
Rice, Lafayette W.
Rice, Archy S.
Reser, Marselles, mustered out Oct. 27, '64.
Ross, William W., mustered out Oct. 27, '64.
Roszell, Thomas, veteranized.
Smith, Parker.
Stegamiller, William F., veteran.

Stricker, Michael W., discharged Nov. 27, '62.
Stricker, Peter, discharged Nov. 26, '62.
Sprigerhoff, Frederick, mustered out Oct. 27, '64.
Taturn, Samuel, discharged Feb. 12, '63.
Tincher, Robert, mustered out Oct. 27, '64.
Tumelty, John, transferred to V. R. C.
Underwood, Nathan, mustered out Oct. 27, '64.
Ummensetts, John, mustered out Oct. 27, '64.
Utt, Andrew J., discharged March 5, '63.
Vogan, George W., veteranized.
Warg, Silas, mustered out Oct. 27, '64.
Whitcomb, Lyman, veteranized.
Wheeler, James H., mustered out Oct. 27, '64.
Wiley, Jerome B., died at Shelbyville, Tenn., June 13, '63.

Enlisted Men of Co. D.

First Sergeant—
Pye, William H., promoted Second Lieutenant.
Sergeants—
Cowan, George W., promoted Second Lieutenant.
Vansickle, Andrew, discharged May 15, '63, disability.
Johnson, David L., discharged Sept. 16, '63, disability.
Stuart, Jasper, mustered out Oct. 27, '64.
Corporals—
Wilson, Robert P., transferred to Tel. Sig. Corps Oct 22, '63.
Hamilton, Thomas, discharged April 24, '63, disability.
Craig, John P., discharged May 2, '62, disability.
Loughridge, Henry B., mustered out Oct. 27, '64.
Lowe, Simon D., killed at Wartrace, Tenn., Sept. 2, '63.
Day, Mahlon, veteranized.
Andrews, Isaac H., veteranized.
Musicians—
Babcock, Monroe, discharged Jan. 17, '63.

Dickson. Newton, veteranized.

Wagoner—
  Piles, John, mustered out Oct. 27, '64.

Privates—
  Andrews, Joseph, discharged Oct. '61.
  Ash, George W., discharged Dec. 27, '62, disability.
  Abbott, Junius, transferred to Fourth U. S. Cavalry.
  Burns, Montalban, died at Bacon creek, Kentucky, Feb. 21, '62.
  Buchanan, George, mustered out Oct. 27, '64.
  Buchanan, John, veteranized.
  Brown, Marion, discharged Jan. 5, '63, disability.
  Brown, Harrison, veteran.
  Brown, James P., veteran.
  Callicott, Henry L., died at Elizabethtown, Ky., Dec. 14, '62.
  Cady, Maly S., discharged May 15, '63, disability.
  Coony, John, veteranized.
  Clark, John, transferred to Fourth U. S. Cavalry Nov. 27, '62.
  Cochran, Levi, veteranized.
  Colles, John, veteranized.
  Crain, Cornelius E., veteranized.
  Cruser, Christian, died at Nashville Nov. 22, '62.
  Corbin, Philip, veteranized.
  Caplinger, Henry, veteranized.
  Davis, Gilford D., veteranized.
  Denny, Charles C., died at Nashville Nov. 17, '62.
  Dearinger, Francis M., discharged Aug. 20, '63, disability.
  Davis, William C., discharged April 7, '63, disability.
  Edens, Ezekiel, veteranized.
  French, Thomas, veteranized.
  Francisco, Obediah A., veteranized.
  Gallager, Alexander, veteranized.

Gray, Thomas, veteranized.
Gaskins, Thomas B., mustered out Oct. 7, '64.
Griffith, William, died May 7, '62.
Hall, Silas, killed at Stone river Dec. 31, '62.
Hall, George, mustered out Oct. 27, '64.
Hallett, John, veteranized.
Hull, Oran, discharged June 11, '62, disability.
Hoffmaster, Frederick, veteranized
Hamilton, Joseph, died at Huntsville, Ala., June 9, '62.
Hamilton, William, veteranized.
Hollensbee, Edward, veteranized.
Hanna, David, veteranized.
Jones, Stephen, veteranized.
Knowlton, Samuel, mustered out Oct. 27, '64.
Lawrence, Thomas, killed in action at Big Shanty, Ga., June 3, '64.
Lutz, Abraham, mustered out Oct. 27, '64
Lowe, Lewis, veteranized.
Love, George W., veteranized.
Leads, James, wounded at Pumpkinvine, captured and died at Atlanta, Ga.
Lockridge, Moody J., mustered out Oct. 27, '64.
McCuen, Arthur Sr., discharged Feb. 4, '63, disability.
McCuen, Arthur Jr., killed at Stone river Dec 31, '62.
Morgan, Warren, veteranized.
Martin, Jeremiah, discharged Dec. 5, '61, disability.
McNew, John J., veteranized.
May, John R., mustered out Oct. 27, '64.
Meulbarger, William H., mustered out Oct. 27, '64.
Munger, Washington, died at Louisville, Ky., Feb. 3, '63.
Newberry, Granville, veteranized.
Oliver, Nicholas, killed at Stone river Dec. 31, '62.
Packett, Benjamin, died at Louisville, Ky., April 16, '62.
Redlon, Eben, died at Louisville, Ky., Jan. 11, '62.

Ruby, John P., mustered out Oct. 27, '64.
Robert, James, mustered out Oct. 27, '64.
Robert, John, mustered out Oct. 27, '64.
Risinger, Washington, died at Bacon creek, Kentucky, Jan. 5, '62.
Sanders, George, veteranized.
Starkey, Thomas, veteranized.
Shook, Jeremiah D., mustered out Oct. 27, '64.
Smallwood, James, died at Elizabethtown, Ky., June 1, '62.
Stevens, Benjamin, veteranized.
Stevens, William.
Stevens, Isaac, mustered out Oct. 27, '64.
Snedaker, Christian, mustered out Oct. 27, '64.
Stark, Thomas, veteranized.
Stark, Benjamin, veteranized.
Signer, William C., died at Nashville, Tenn., April 8, '62.
Suits, Charles C., died at Shelbyville, Tenn., June 20, '62.
Sage, Elihu, veteranized.
Thackery, William B., discharged Nov. 27, '62, disability.
Thackery, Selecter, mustered out Oct. 27, '64.
Vankirk, William, mustered out Oct. 27, '64.
Whitaker, John, died at Olean, Ind., April 18, '62.
Webster, Lysander, transferred to V. R. C.
Wagoner, Jacob, transferred to Fourth U. S. Cavalry.
Wise, James, mustered out Oct. 27, '64.
Wehr, Joshua, mustered out Oct. 27, '64.

Enlisted Men of Co. E.

First Sergeant—
  Harvey, William B., promoted Adjutant.
Sergeants—
  Ford, Lafayette, mustered out Oct. 27, '64.

Perry, Thomas B., discharged Aug. 8, '63.
Raynes, Will A., died at Elizabethtown, Ky., Dec. 30, '61.
Hungate, George W., promoted Second Lieutenant.

Corporals—
Whitlow, William A., transferred to V. R. C. Nov. 1, '63.
Guthrie, Philip S., died at Bacon creek, Kentucky, Feb. 13, '62.
Ballard, Daniel J., mustered out Oct. 27, '64.
Cook, Abraham B., veteranized.
Sherman, Charles W., discharged May 26, '63.
Sidener, Martin F., discharged June 1, '62.
Gully, James W., discharged Jan. 1, '63.
Barnes, Wesley N., discharged Jan. 1, '63.

Musicians—
Butler, Nicholas A., died at Washington, D. C., Oct. 22, '62.
Stopper, William, veteranized.

Wagoner—
Price, Benjamin F., mustered out Oct. 27, '64.

Privates—
Adkins, James G., mustered out Oct. 27, '64.
Adkins, Wesley H., discharged Jan. 20, '63.
Ballard, Columbus, transferred to V. R. C. Nov. 1, 1863.
Barton, Joshua, mustered out Oct. 27, '64, Corporal.
Beck, Frederick, veteranized.
Bowling, Hiram, mustered out Oct. 27, '64.
Brooks, Martin, died at Macon, Ga., Aug. 20, '62.
Brooks, Lewis C., veteranized.
Bullington, George W., mustered out Oct. 27, '64.
Buell, Matthew, discharged July 12, '62, disability.
Carter, Thomas H., mustered out Oct. 27, '64.
Clark, William E., discharged Feb. 4, '63.
Connet, Albert B., mustered out Oct. 27, '64.

Cook, Andrew J., veteranized.
Coleman, Edward, discharged Nov. 12, '62.
Conner, Reuben H., discharged June 1, '62.
Conner, James R., killed in battle May 9, '62.
Cox, James, mustered out Oct. 27, '64.
Christler, William J., mustered out Oct. 27, '64.
Creed, Howard, mustered out Oct. 27, '64.
Davidson, Samuel, mustered out Oct. 27, '64.
Deen, William, died at Bacon creek, Ky., Feb. 22, '62.
Engsminger, Andrew, mustered out Oct. 27, '64.
Eubanks, George H., mustered out Oct. 27, '64.
Favour, Robert, mustered out Oct. 27, '64.
Fleming, George W., discharged July 27, '63.
Ford, Joseph, mustered out Oct. 27, '64.
Ford, Benjamin F., mustered out Oct. 27, '64.
Garrett, Oscar M., discharged Jan. 27, '63.
Glass, John T., mustered out Oct. 27, '64.
Gullion, George W., mustered out Oct. 27, '64.
Hanger, James A.
Heaton, Robert F., killed in battle May 9, '62.
Hogan, Henry, mustered out Oct. 27, '64.
Hogan, Charles, died Oct. 19, '62.
Hornice, Gideon, mustered out Oct. 27, '64.
Hughes, Addison, mustered out Oct. 27, '64.
Hunt, Charles T., discharged July 12, '62.
Johnson, James T., mustered out Oct. 27, '64.
Jordon, James, killed in battle May 9, '62.
Knapp, Abram, veteranized.
Knight, Thaddeus V., discharged Jan. 22, '63.
Lewis, Stephen, discharged Nov. 30, '62.
Lewis, James C., discharged Jan. 6, '64.
Martin, Milton, veteranized.
Marsh, Willard R., mustered out Oct. 27, '64.
Maharry, Jacob, died at Murfreesboro in April 1, '63.
Marks, Jos. A., died at Elizabethtown, Ky., Dec. 18, '61.

McKeeon, William, veteranized.
McKee, James C., veteranized.
McNeely, Bert, veteranized.
Morgan, John T., killed in battle May 9, '62.
Neeb, Jacob W., discharged Nov. 27, '62.
Parson, John, mustered out Oct. 27, '64, Corporal.
Price, Dudley, mustered out Oct. 27, '64.
Richy, William, died at Chattanooga, Tenn., Aug. 10, '64.
Ricketts, Enoch, discharged.
Scull, Arthur O., mustered out Oct. 27, '64.
Scull, Alfred C., killed in battle May 9, '64.
Slifer, Philip, mustered out Oct. 27, '64.
Slifer, John, mustered out Oct. 27, '64.
Smawley, Reuben, died at Bacon creek, Kentucky, Feb. 13, '62.
Smawley, Lewis, discharged Dec. 1, '63.
Smith, John H., discharged Aug. 11, '62.
Smith, Benjamin R., discharged Jan. 2, '64.
Stogsdell, John B., died at Macon, Ga., Oct. 14, '64.
Stark, Bethuel G., mustered out Oct. 27, '64.
Swango, Solomon, mustered out Oct. 27, '64.
Tevis, Thomas S., died at Charlotte, N. C., Oct. 12, '62.
Tillison, James, discharged Aug. 1, wounds received in battle.
Thompson, William H., mustered out Oct. 27, '64.
Tractwell, James, died at Elizabethtown, Ky., Dec. 19, '61.
Walker, Lafayette, mustered out Oct. 27, '64.
Wells, Samuel, mustered out Oct. 27, '64.
Whitlow, Buckner C., discharged Aug. 1, '62, wounds received in battle.
Wilson, Milton M., veteranized.
Wimber, James, died at Bacon creek, Kentucky, Dec. 30, '61.

Wilder, Wesley, mustered out Oct. 27, '64.
Wooley, James H., veteranized.
Wooters, Albert, died at Bacon creek, Kentucky, Jan. 9, '62.
Wolverton, John F., veteranized.
Wood, Thomas J., veteranized.

Recruits—
  Stevens, Thomas J., transferred V. R. C.
  Scott, Samuel, transferred Thirty-seventh Regiment re-organized.
  Woodard, Charles W., transferred Thirty-seventh Regiment re-organized.

Enlisted Men of Co. F.

First Sergeant—
  Speer, William, promoted Second Lieutenant.
Sergeants—
  Hoover, William I., mustered out Oct. 27, '64, as Commissary Sergeant.
  Barnhart, Joseph I., mustered out Oct. 27, '64.
  Passel, James L., veteran, promoted Captain U. S. C. T.
  Cole, Eleazer, mustered out Oct. 27, '64, as First Sergeant.
Corporals—
  Wallace, William H., mustered out Oct. 27, '64.
  Spencer, John F., mustered out Oct. 27, '64.
  Richardson, Josiah, mustered out Oct. 27, '64, as First Sergeant.
  Hoover, George S., died at Dillsborough April 21, '63.
  Hundley, William, mustered out Oct. 27, '64.
  Gray, James, mustered out Oct. 27, '64.
  Ayers, William, died at Dillsborough March 31, '62.
  Pearson, John, mustered out Oct. 27, '64.
Musicians—
  Meyer, Adam, mustered out Oct. 27, '64.

Shott, Ezekiel, discharged Jan. 29. '63, disability.
Wagoner—
Shutts, Aaron, discharged April '63, disability.
Privates—
Ard, Jacob, mustered out Oct. 27, '64.
Acre, Thomas, discharged July 31, '62, disability.
Busby, John P., mustered out Oct. 27, '64.
Beall, Isaac, mustered out Oct. 27, '64.
Beck, Foster, mustered out Oct. 27, '64.
Burroughs, James L., killed at Stone river Dec. 31, '62.
Burroughs, George, discharged Feb. 20, '63, wounds.
Bruce, John T.
Beall, John, died at Louisville, Ky., March 3, '63.
Carnine, James M., mustered out Oct. 27, '64.
Craven, Henry, killed at Stone river Dec. 31, '62.
Daniel, James, mustered out Oct. 27, '64.
Danfort, Robert, discharged June 18, '62, disability.
Gordon, William H., mustered out Oct. 27, '64.
Green, William, discharged Sept. 16, '63, disability.
Gankroger, Hartley, transferred to V. R. C.
Gloyd, William, died.
Goddart, John F., killed at Stone river Dec. 31, '62.
Headly, George, discharged April 13, '63, disability.
Hess, Matthias, discharged April 17, '63, disability.
Hair, David H., mustered out Oct. 27, '64.
Herndon, Samuel, died at Nashville, Tenn., Jan. 16, '63, wounds.
Hess, Samuel W., died at Nashville, Tenn., Sept. 8, '62, wounds.
Heaton, John P., mustered out Oct. 27, '64.
Jennings, Thomas A., mustered out Oct. 27, '64.
Knowles, Robert T., discharged, disability.
Knowles, William F., discharged July 28, '62, disability.
Kirk, John J., mustered out Oct. 27, '64.

Kincaid, George, discharged Aug. 7, '62, disability.
Kolkmire, Henry, discharged Oct. 18, '62, disability.
Kile, John H., died at Nashville, Tenn., Oct. 28, '62.
Lenover, George, mustered out Oct. 27, '64.
Lemon, John T., discharged April 17, '63, disability.
Lenover, Benjamin, killed at Dallas, Ga., May 27, '64.
Lazure, Elias, discharged March 12, '63, disability.
Leiker, William F., discharged Nov. 29, '62.
Mitchell, George S., discharged March 5, '63, disability.
Morford, Squire T., discharged Feb. 6, '62, disability.
Martin, John, discharged Jan. 14, '63, disability.
Morgan, Jacob S., discharged April 17, '63, disability.
Martin, Solon, died at Louisville, Ky., March 7, '62.
Munson, Alfred G.
McDonald, Philip.
Newberry, Edward, mustered out Oct. 27, '64.
Parker, John, died at Bacon creek, Kentucky, Jan. 5, '62.
Palmer, John, died at Jeffersonville, Ind., June 15, '64.
Palmer, James, died at Chattanooga, Tenn., June 11, '64.
Palmer, Stephen W., mustered out Oct. 27, '64.
Proctor, Thomas, mustered out Oct. 27, '64.
Roberts, Leroy, mustered out Oct. 27, '64.
Rowland, William, discharged March 30, '63, wounds.
Ruble, George, mustered out Oct. 27, '64.
Roberts, Samuel, mustered out Oct. 27, '64.
Spencer, Augustus E., died at Tullahoma, Tenn., Aug. 8, '63.
Smith, John G., mustered out Oct. 27, '64.
Shutts, James H., mustered out Oct. 27, '64.
Shutts, Abram, discharged May 27, '64.
Sanks, George W., mustered out Oct. 27, '64.
Sprong, William H., died at Gallatin, Tenn., Jan. 13, '63.

Sanks, Daniel, killed at Stone river Dec. 31, '62.
Sweazy, John M., veteran, transferred to U. S. Engineer July 24, '64.
Smith, Samuel C., killed at Stone river Dec. 31, '62.
Smith, Charles B., died at Elizabethtown, Ky., Dec. 11, '61.
Shepherd, John M., died at Huntsville, Ala., May 11, '62.
Stafford, John, discharged Nov. 25, '62.
Stewart, Charles, killed at Stone river Dec. 31, '62.
Shipman, William H., mustered out Oct. 27, '64.
Shull, William J., died Jan. 2, '63, wounds.
Teake, John, mustered out Oct. 27, '64.
Tate, George discharged July 31, '62, disability.
Thomas, Thomas, mustered out Oct. 27, '64.
Vandolah, Joseph C., mustered out Oct. 27, '64.
Vidito, Willis, mustered out Oct. 27, '64.
Vandolah, Joseph, mustered out Oct. 27, '64, prisoner.
Withrow, John Q. A., mustered out Oct. 27, '64.
Wilson, John, mustered out Oct. 27, '64.
Wilson, William T., mustered out Oct. 27, '64, Corporal.
Warner, Marcus D., mustered out Oct. 27, '64.
White, William, died at Nashville, Tenn., Jan. 17, '63.
Winter, Henry F., mustered out Oct. 27, '64.
Weitzel, Henry M., mustered out Oct. 27, '64.

Recruits—
Brumley, Charles W., died at Nashville, Tenn., Jan. 31, '62.
Godert, John G., killed at Dallas, Ga., May 27, '64.
Maritz, William K., discharged Feb. 3, '63, disability.
Shedrick, Johnson, died at Murfreesboro July 24, '64.

Enlisted Men of Co. G.

First Sergeant—
DeArmond, James M.

Sergeants—
  Baughman, William H., promoted Second Lieutenant.
  Lee, Aaron S., mustered out Oct. 27, '64.
  Hetrick, John S., mustered out Oct. 27, '64.
  Clendening, James S., died in Kentucky Jan. 13, '62.
Corporals—
  Bartow, John W., mustered out Oct. 27, '64.
  Gray, John M., discharged Feb. 6, '63, disability.
  Gray, Philetus M., died at Nashville, Tenn., Feb. 13, '63.
  Hinds, James J., discharged Sept. 23, '64.
  Keen, Peter, killed at Stone river Dec. 31, '62.
  Bayles, Samuel R., mustered out Oct. 27, '64.
  Baker, Oliver B., mustered out Oct. 27, '64.
  Bowe, Samuel B., mustered out Oct. 27, '64.
Musicians—
  Fox, John H., veteranized.
  Shields, Samuel C., mustered out Oct. 27, '64.
Wagoner—
  Keeler, Ira M., veteranized.
Privates—
  Allen, Robert, discharged March 14, '63, disability.
  Anthony, Henry, died at Murfreesboro, Tenn., April 9, '63.
  Armstrong, James T., mustered out Oct. 27, '64.
  Abbott, Oscar, died at Louisville, Ky., Jan. 12, '62.
  Adams, Charles G., mustered out Oct. 27, '64.
  Adams, Wilson W., discharged Oct. 4, '62, disability.
  Barbour, Samuel, discharged Feb. 19, '63, disability.
  Brady, Isaac N., died at Springfield, Ind., Feb. 27, '63.
  Burk, Coleman S., died June 6, '64, of wounds received at Dallas, Ga.
  Bals, Philip, discharged Nov. 27, '62.
  Cochran, William H., mustered out Oct. 27, '64.
  Clendening, Adison W., died in Kentucky Jan. 5, '62.

Conery, Dennis W., died Jan. 27, '63, of wounds received at Stone river.
Coen, Marion, discharged Jan. 30, '63.
Craig, William R., killed at Stone river Dec. 31, '62.
Eckley, Edward, discharged July 14, '62.
Fisher, James A., veteranized.
Finley, George W., discharged March 26, '63, disability.
Gamber, John, veteranized.
Gray, David H., mustered out Oct. 27, '64.
Greenlee, James S., veteranized.
Golladay, Thomas T., died at Nashville, Tenn., March 25, '63.
Goshorn, Wilson N., mustered out Oct. 27, '64.
Glisson, Elisha E., killed at Dallas, Ga., May 27, '64.
George, Atwell, veteranized.
Gordon, Frank, discharged in August, '62.
Hinds, Benjamin F., mustered out Oct. 27, '64.
Hamlin, John, veteranized.
Hannah, William T., died at Elizabethtown, Ky., Nov. 22, '61.
Hannah, Thomas C., mustered out Oct. 27, '64.
Kelly, William, veteranized.
Kelly, Ellis, mustered out Oct. 27, '64.
Keeler, John M., veteranized.
Kennedy, John A., mustered out Oct. 27, '64.
Liming, William, veteranized.
Luse, Robert H., discharged Sept. 4, '63, disability.
Lynch, John P., mustered out Oct. 27, '64.
Millspaugh, William, mustered out Oct. 27, '64.
McCaw, James S., mustered out Oct. 27, '64.
Mathews, Henry P., mustered out Oct. 27, '64.
Maddin, John, mustered out Oct. 27, '64.
Miller, John, veteranized.
Miles, William, mustered out Oct. 27, '64.

Proctor, Abram, mustered out Oct. 27, '64.
Roberts, William F., mustered out Oct. 27, '64.
Rowe, James P., mustered out Oct. 27, '64.
Reynolds, William M., mustered out Oct. 27, '64.
Scott, Joseph, veteranized.
Stone, Henry, mustered out Oct. 27, '64.
Scofield, Edward, veteranized.
Stout, Jefferson M., died at Louisville, Ky., Jan. 27, '62.
Small, Edward, discharged May 26, '63, disability.
Sutton, William, killed at Stone river Dec. 31, '62.
Souter, Oswell, mustered out Oct. 27, '64.
Sickler, George M., mustered out Oct. 27, '64.
Snoddy, Robert J., mustered out Oct. 27, '64.
Selfridge, William R., mustered out Oct. 27, '64.
Sizelone, Joseph R., veteranized.
Schaub, Frank, died at Louisville, Ky., Jan. 25, '62.
True, Thomas F., veteranized.
Thomas, Lewis, died at Louisville, Ky., Jan. 20, '62.
Taylor, Squire A., transferred to Co. B Thirty-seventh Regiment re-organized.
Viley, Isaac, mustered out Oct. 27, '64.
Woodapple, Charles E., discharged Jan. 20, '63.
Weeks, John.
Wood, John, discharged July 9, '62, disability.
White, Eber C., mustered out Oct. 27, '64.
Welch, John, discharged Nov. 27, '62.
Young, Charles J., mustered out Oct. 27, '64.
Zink, William H., mustered out Oct. 27, '64.
Zubrick, John, mustered out Oct. 27, '64.

Recruits—

  Bartlow, William H., transferred to Co. B Thirty-seventh Regiment re-organized.

  Hetrick, James W., discharged April 21, '63, disability.

  Hamlin, Omer, transferred to Co. B Thirty-seventh Regiment re-organized.

Larue, George N., transferred to Co. B Thirty-seventh Regiment re-organized.
Lowes, Cyrenus S., transferred to Co. B Thirty-seventh Regiment re-organized.
Millspaugh, George C., transferred to Co. B Thirty-seventh Regiment re-organized.
Shafer, Henry J., transferred to Co. B Thirty-seventh Regiment re-organized.
Vaness, Ephraim, discharged Nov. 27, '62.

Enlisted Men of Co. H.

First Sergeant—
  Burk, James H., died at Nashville, Tenn., July 9, '64, of wounds.
Sergeants—
  Douglas, Jno. S., died at Chattanooga, Tenn., June 15, '6:
  Smith, Levi, dropped from the rolls Oct. 31, '62.
  Fowler, Benjamin D., mustered out Oct. 27, '64.
  Hice, John L., promoted First Lieutenant
Corporals—
  Tevis, Augustus H., promoted Second Lieutenant.
  Proctor, Joel M., killed at Dallas, Ga., May 27, '64.
  Jones, John, died at Bowling Green, Ky., March 14, '6:
  Paul, John J., died at Camp Jackson, Tenn. March 5, '62.
  Roop, John M., discharged Feb. 9, '63, wounds.
  Sutton, David B., mustered out Oct. 27, '64.
  Jackson, Cyrus A., discharged Oct. 4, '64, wounds.
  Garrison, Joseph W., transferred to V. R. C. Jan 15, '6:
Musicians—
  Tyner, Isaac J., discharged June 5, '62, disability.
  Cunningham, James J., transferred to V. R. C May 15, '64.
Wagoner—
  Moor, Milton G., mustered out Oct. 27, '64.

Privates—
Brunton, Noah L., mustered out Oct. 27, '64.
Burk, William H., dropped from rolls Oct. 31, '62.
Burk, Newton, discharged Dec. 1, '62, disability.
Baldwin, William, transferred to Fourth U. S. Cavalry.
Buck, James, died at Nashville, Tenn., Jan. 16, '63, wounds.
Cowen, Squire H., mustered out Oct. 27, '64.
Cowen, Harrison, mustered out Oct. 27, '64.
Cowen, John, mustered out Oct. 27, '64.
Clark, Benjamin F., veteranized.
Davis, Edward, discharged Nov. 27, '62, to enlist in U. S. Cavalry.
Dickson, Samuel, discharged June 3, '62, disability.
Day, James C., discharged April 27, '63, disability.
Douglas, David, mustered out Oct. 27, '64.
Demoss, Benjamin L., died at Murfreesboro May 4, '63.
Day, Henry, died at Murfreesboro March 12, '63.
Daily, Barton N., veteranized.
Diggs, George C. W., died at Bowling Green, Ky., March 2, '62.
Enos, Stephen, transferred V. R. C. Nov. 15, '63.
Ewbanks, Robert, discharged March 27, '63, disability.
Ford, William S., dropped from rolls Oct. 31, '62.
Ford, Thomas S., died at Louisville, Ky., Feb. 19, '63.
Ferguson, James P., mustered out Oct. 27, '64.
Fredinburg, Hiram, died at Evansville, Ind., Nov. 4, '63.
Fry, Alfred, mustered out Oct. 27, '64.
Harper, Samuel, dropped from rolls Oct. 31, '63.
Hunter, Lewis M., mustered out Oct. 27, '64.
Hoter, John, discharged Dec. 20, '62, disability.
Hutchison, Jacob A., died at Murfreesboro Feb. 11, '63.
Hunter, John, mustered out Oct. 27, '64.
Harry, Daniel, discharged Sept. 10, '63, disability.

Homsher, William, mustered out Oct. 27, '64.
Harrell, William, mustered out Oct. 27, '64.
Harrell, John S., discharged Oct. 18, '61, disability.
Johnston, John A., mustered out Oct. 27, '64.
Laforge, William, died at Camp Jefferson, Ky., Jan. 5, '62.
Moor, Martin, mustered out Oct. 27, '64.
McCracken, Francis F., discharged March 25, '63, wounds.
Miller, Samuel, transferred to V. R. C. Nov. 21, '63.
Martin, Richard, dropped from rolls Oct. 31, '63.
Murray, William R., killed at Murfreesboro, Ky., Dec. 31, '62.
Miller, James, discharged Nov. 28, '62, to enlist in U. S. Cavalry.
McClure, Samuel M., promoted Assistant Surgeon.
Mitchell, James T., discharged Oct. 18, '62, disability.
Owen, Anderson, mustered out Oct. 27, '64.
Patrick, Warren, discharged Jan. 14, '63, disability.
Patrick, Elisha G., died at Huntsville, Ala., July 13, '62.
Patrick, James, discharged Dec. 4, '62, disability.
Pettit, James, discharged Aug. 5, '62.
Peak, James W., killed at Dallas, Ga., May 27, '64.
Robbins, Absalom, dropped from rolls Oct. 31, '62.
Robbins, Harrison, killed at Murfreesboro Dec. 31, '62.
Rutherford, Anderson, veteranized.
Stonecypher, David, discharged June 6, '62, disability.
Shattuck, Nathaniel, mustered out Oct. 27, '64.
Stout, Theodore L., dropped from rolls Oct. 31, '62.
Scott, James R., died at Nashville, Tenn., Oct. 9, '62.
Shafer, William G., transferred to V. R. C. April 30, '62.
Shera, Thomas W., died at Murfreesboro May 4, '63.
Starrett, Benjamin, discharged July 9, '62.
Shirk, Thomas A., mustered out Oct. 27, '64, as Sergeant.

INDIANA VOLUNTEER INFANTRY. 173

Shaw, Zemry. died at Murfreesboro April 11, '62.
Steward, Henry J., mustered out Oct. 27. '64.
Snook, Martin J.. mustered out Oct. 27. '64.
Thompson, William A.. discharged Oct. 24, '63, wounds.
Waggoner, Andrew, dropped from rolls.
Williams, Samuel. killed at Murfreesboro Dec. 31. '62.
Watson, Alfred. died at Chattanooga July 24, '64, wounds.
Woodall, John D., discharged Aug. 27, '62, disability.
Wimmer, John C., discharged June 20, '62, disability.
Whittaker, Robert, discharged May 12, '63, disability.
Yauger, Isaac, discharged Sept. 25, '61, disability.
Recruits—
  Denham, Benjamin T., transferred to Thirty-seventh Regiment re-organized.
  Denham, James B., transferred to Thirty-seventh Regiment re-organized.
  Ward, James, transferred to Thirty-seventh Regiment re-organized.

Enlisted Men of Co. I.

First Sergeant—
  Myers, George W., promoted Second Lieutenant.
Sergeants—
  Bodine, Jeremiah M., veteranized.
  Huff, Robert B.. died at Murfreesboro Jan. 23, '63, wounds.
  Bodine, William A.. discharged Oct. 9, '63, disability.
  Dunn, Isacc M., died at Louisville, Ky.
Corporals—
  Meyer, Jacob. mustered out Oct. 27, '64, as First Sergeant.
  Bachert, Joseph, veteranized.
  Pernell, Robert K., veteranized.
  Ong, Theodore W.. mustered out Oct. 27, '64.

Cox, Eli, mustered out Oct. 27, '64.
Owen, John J., veteranized.
Jones, James B., discharged March 23, '63, disability.
White, Thomas J., veteranized.

Musicians—
Pierce, John D., veteranized.
Christopher, Michael J., veteranized.

Wagoner—
Harry, James, veteranized.

Privates—
Abercrombie, William.
Amon, Frederick, veteranized.
Alfred, Joshua, died June 27, '64, wounds.
Bodine, James A., mustered out Oct. 27, '64.
Burlbaw, John, veteranized.
Burgdurfer, Louis, mustered out Oct. 27, '64.
Burlbaw, Nicholas, mustered out Oct. 27, '64.
Burchard, John H., discharged Oct. 18, '61.
Brasher, Robert W., discharged July 22, '63.
Childers, Ezekiel, discharged.
Cross, James H., killed at Dallas May 27, '64.
Cuppy, Henry H., mustered out Oct. 27, '64.
Carpenter, Oliver, veteranized.
Cox, Thomas J. No. 1, mustered out Oct. 27, '64.
Camron, John, veteranized.
Cox, Thomas J. No. 2, mustered out Oct. 27, '64.
Cox, William A., veteranized.
DeArmond, Alfred.
Dove, Isaac.
Dunn, Samuel H., veteranized.
Davis, Mansion, died Nov. 18, '64, wounds.
Gibson, Charles H., veteranized.
Goss, Andrew A., discharged Dec. 9, '62, disability.
Gordon, John.
Hennecy, John, mustered out Oct. 27, '64.

Hough, Daniel L., discharged in January, '64.
Harrison, Levi, veteranized.
Johnson, Charles F., veteranized.
Johnson, Jacob.
Jones, Reuben, killed at Stone river Dec. 31. '62.
Kennedy, John, veteranized.
Kelly, Barnard, veteranized.
Longely, Peter, veteranized.
Lofland, Littleton, discharged May 18. '63, disability.
Larman, Frederick.
McClelland, Francis M., discharged Jan. 23, '62, disability.
McKinney, Michael, discharged Nov. 27,' 62, disability.
Martin, Eleazer, died at Chattanooga, Tenn., June 19, '64, wounds.
Morris, Levi, mustered out Oct. 27. '64.
Martin, Sterling A., discharged.
Maple, Ephraim B., discharged July 9, '62, disability.
Massey, Drewney A., mustered out Oct. 27, '64.
McWethy, N. Jerome, died at Murfreesboro Jan. 23, '63.
Mitchel, George H., died at Camp Jefferson, Ky.,
Nelson, Derastus W., veteranized.
North, Thomas J., mustered out Oct. 27. '64.
Nulker, Joseph, mustered out Oct. 27, '64.
Payne, William, veteranized.
Powell, John, veteranized.
Rees, Tyre, died at Camp Jefferson, Ky., Dec. 7. '61.
Straight, William H., veteranized.
Stoll, John G., veteranized.
Stowbridge, Daniel O., mustered out Oct. 27. '64.
Shaw, Joshua, died at Murfreesboro Jan. 17, '63.
Shiveley, William H., discharged Nov. 27. '64.
Spears, John, veteranized.
Salls, Daniel, discharged June 23. '62.
Shoure, Joseph.

Snyder, John, veteranized.
Smith, John W., discharged.
Smith Eppenetus, mustered out Oct. 27, '64.
Thorp, Marcus L., mustered out Oct. 27, '64.
Tucker, William, discharged April 22, '63, disability.
Travilian, William, discharged Nov. 27, '62, disability.
Taylor, John.
Turk, Samuel H., discharged Dec. 10, '62.
Widener, Abram T., veteranized.
Widener, Leonard, veteranized.
Williamson, John, veteranized.
Whitcomb, Lewis, discharged Jan. 23, '63, disability.

Recruits—
  Bohlander, John, transferred to Co. A Thirty-seventh Regiment re-organized.
  Critchlow, Evans, transferred to Co. A Thirty-seventh Regiment re-organized.
  Dalrymple, Charles L., transferred to Co. A Thirty-seventh Regiment re-organized.
  Hornung, Lewis, transferred to Co. A Thirty-seventh Regiment re-organized.
  Hornung, Andrew, transferred to Co. A Thirty-seventh Regiment re-organized.
  Kinney, John, transferred to Co. A Thirty-seventh Regiment re-organized.
  Linville, Thomas, transferred to Co. A Thirty-seventh Regiment re-organized.
  Long, John, died at Bacon creek, Kentucky, Dec. 7, '61.
  Maynard, Henry, transferred to Co. A Thirty-seventh Regiment re-organized.
  Mulkins, James H., died June 19, '64, of wounds.
  Redlow, Daniel M., promoted Quartermaster Sergeant.
  Somerville, James W., transferred to Co. A Thirty-seventh Regiment re-organized.
  Uppinghouse, Eli F., transferred to Co. A Thirty-

seventh Regiment re-organized.

Uppinghouse, John B., transferred to Co. A Thirty-seventh Regiment re-organized.

Enlisted Men of Co. K.

First Sergeant—
  Patton, John, died of wounds received at Stone river Feb. 13, '63.
Sergeants—
  Danner, Samuel T., discharged Aug. 7, '63.
  Puntenney, George H., mustered out Oct. 27, '64, as Sergeant Major.
  Lingenfelter, John F., died at Bowling Green, Ky., Feb. 23, '62.
  Hunt, William R., promoted First Lieutenant.
Corporals—
  Schwartz, David, discharged Dec. 29, '63.
  Stewart, John M., killed at Dallas May 27, '64.
  Plough, William J., transferred to V. R. C. Feb. 11, '64.
  Elstun, Marion, died of wounds at Vining Station, Ga., July 23, '64.
  Cowan, Elbert N., mustered out Oct. 27, '64.
  Rankins, James W., killed at Peach Tree creek July 20, '64.
  Richey, Jasper, mustered out Oct. 27, '64.
  Cowan, Robert, discharged March 18, '63, disability.
Musicians—
  Bastian, Sibrant, veteranized.
  Butler, James S., transferred V. R. C.
Wagoner—
  O'Brien, James, mustered out Oct. 27, '64.
Privates—
  Brown, John E., mustered out Oct. 24, '64.
  Blair, Joseph, mustered out Oct. 24, '64.
  Black, Jeremiah, mustered out Oct. 24, '64.

Bowlby, Mahlon L., mustered out Oct. 24, '64.
Boylan, Thomas, mustered out Oct. 27, '64, as Musician.
Boling, William C., mustered out Oct. 27, '64.
Cowan, John A., mustered out Oct. 27, '64.
Culver, John W., transferred to Signal Corps Jan. 13, '64.
Clemonts, Joseph, mustered out Oct. 27, '64.
Davis, Elbert H., mustered out Oct. 27, '64.
Davis, John W., mustered out Oct. 27, '64, as Corporal.
Davis, John W. B., mustered out Oct. 27, '64.
Elliott, John L., mustered out Oct. 27, '64.
Endicott, John T., mustered out Oct. 27, '64.
Gabal, Fielding, died at Decherd, Tenn., Aug. 8, '62.
Glass, Lowry M., died at Louisville, Ky., Jan. 20, '62.
Glass, Samuel, mustered out Oct. 27, '64, as Corporal.
Holmes, Alexander, mustered out Oct. 27, '64.
Harrison, Isaac N., mustered out Oct. 27, '64.
Hall, James M., mustered out Oct. 27, '64.
Hudelson, Rufus L., mustered out Oct. 27, '64.
Hudelson, William H., discharged, disability.
Huston, William R., mustered out Oct. 27, '64.
Hemerly, Wilbur W., died at Louisville, Ky., Jan. 8, 62.
Jones, Erastus T., died at Bacon creek, Kentucky, Jan. 21, '62.
Jackson, Henry, mustered out Oct. 27, '64.
Jones, William B., discharged, disability.
Junkin, Washington, transferred V. R. C. Jan. 15, '64.
Kirkem, Andrew B., killed at Stone river Dec. 30, '62.
Kethsel, Jacob, mustered out Oct. 27, '64.
Lindsay, Clinton, mustered out Oct. 27, '64.
Lothridge, James, mustered out Oct. 27, '64.
McClain, Arthur, mustered out Oct. 27, '64, as Corporal.
McCullough, Jacob S., mustered out Oct. 27, '64.

McGhee, James, mustered out Oct. 27, '64.
Mitchell, James W., discharged March 22, '63, wounds.
Morgan, Philip A., mustered out Oct. 27, '64.
McGuiness, Thomas, mustered out Oct. 27, '64.
Mitchell, William T., died at Shelbyville, Tenn., June 14, '62.
Patton, Samuel R., mustered out Oct. 27, '64, as Corporal.
Patton, William C., mustered out Oct. 27, '64.
Rankin, Jeremiah, discharged in March, '62, disability.
Rankin, William R., killed in battle July 21, '64.
Rankin, Samuel A., discharged in March, '62.
Ruddell, James H.
Stewart, David S., mustered out Oct. 27, '64.
Stewart, Harrison, discharged, disability.
Stephens, James M., mustered out Oct. 27, '64.
Stewart, Samuel P., mustered out Oct. 27, '64.
Stewart, William N., mustered out Oct. 27, '64, as Quartermaster Sergeant.
Scott, William H., mustered out Oct. 27, '64, as Sergeant.
Thompson, Robert S., killed in battle at Dallas, Ga., May 27, '63.
Williams, Charles, transferred to V. V. C. Nov. 15, '63.
Wiggins, Henry B., transferred to V. R. C.

Recruits—
  Butler, Alexander S., transferred to Co. B Thirty-seventh Regiment re-organized.
  Buck, William L., died at Murfreesboro, Tenn., May 20, '63.
  Minor, Joseph, mustered out Oct. 27, '64.
  Mitchell, David L., transferred to Co. B Thirty-seventh Regiment re-organized.
  Morelock, John B., died at Murfreesboro, Tenn., of wounds, Jan. 16, '63.

Stewart, Robert C., killed in battle June 18, '64.
Thorn, John D., transferred to Co. B Thirty-seventh Regiment re-organized.

Unassigned Recruits.

Brown, Theodore F.
Bond, Levi L.
Bassett, Lewis.
Daniel, William E.
Davis, Allen.
Davis, Charles L.
Hook, George.
Mitchell, Daniel.
Mullen, James M.
Monroe, Calvin.
Miller, William Harris.
Moore, Craven B.
Sharp, James W.
Scott, James W.
Taten, Samuel A.
Whitcomb, Lewis J.
Yates, John P.

THE MARCH TO THE SEA.

"Sherman's Bummers" Having a High Old Time.

September 19th, 1864, the non-veterans took their departure for Indianapolis. We were loth to part with them, and with sad hearts we watched the old flag as it receded from view toward the rear. We felt that we were orphaned indeed as we bade them a kind adieu.

After the non-veterans had gone home there remained about two hundred and twenty-five men—some of them recruits and some half dozen Lieutenants which were formed into two Companies and a detachment, designated as Co. A and Co. B residuary battalion Thirty-seventh Indiana Veteran Volunteer Infantry. Three of the Lieutenants resigned in a few days and thirteen non-commissioned officers were discharged for the reason that that number were made superfluous by reason of the consolidation of Companies. First Lieutenant John L. Henry was given command of the battalion; Companies A, D and I were consolidated and called Co. A detachment Thirty-seventh Indiana Veteran Volunteer Infantry, with Second Lieutenant George M. Myers in command; Companies B, C and K were consolidated and called Co. B Thirty-seventh Indiana Veteran Volunteer Infantry, with Second Lieutenant Socrates Carver in command. The men of the remaining four Companies were consolidated into a detachment under Sergeant Wolverton, of Co. E. Some of our men were absent, sick and with wounds, a large per cent. were at once detailed in Quartermaster, Commissary and Ordnance departments, and the rest—about eighty men, were detailed as guards to the corps supply train under charge of Capt. Remington. On Oct. 1st sixty of our men went back to Nashville after mules for teams.

Our headquarters remained for some time where the Regiment left us, and taking down some buildings, with the material we had, constructed quite comfortable quarters; but we were not allowed to enjoy them very long, as about this time Hood undertook his memorable campaign on Nashville, which terminated in the destruction of his army. Gen. Thomas, with the Fourth and Twenty-third corps, fell back in advance of Hood, and Gen. Sherman pursued with the rest of the army except the Twentieth corps, which remained at Atlanta. There was but little fighting except at Altoona Pass, where the Johnnies attempted to seize our commissary stores. But Gen. Corse held the fort and the Confederates were severely punished. We came up soon after the battle and assisted in collecting some of the dead and wounded Johnnies whom their friends had left in their haste to get away before being overtaken by our army in their rear. Hood with his army continued north through Kingston, Calhoun, Resaca, and when near Dalton, having destroyed much of the railroad, turned to the left, passed through Snake Creek Gap to Sum-

George W. Eubank, Co. E.
Indianapolis, Ind.

merville, thence into Alabama, our troops closely pursuing. Our wagon train passed through Snake Creek Gap, thence to Mattox Gap, thence down the Chattooga valley to Galesville, Ala. Here Gen. Sherman gave up the pursuit of Hood about the 20th of October, and the army rested about a week. This being a rich valley, much forage and provisions were collected and much destroyed.

From here the army set out again for Atlanta. The first day, after a hard march over a rough country, we reached Rome, Georgia, rested a day or two, then moved on to Kingston, where we remained several days. While here Nov. 8th, the Presidential election was held. All the troops were allowed to vote except those from Indiana, this privilege our patriotic legislature denied us. The next day the paymaster made us a welcome visit and we received several months' pay.

Our next move was to Cartersville, where we re-

T. H. Carter, Co. E.
Moscow, Ind.

mained several days. The railroad had been repaired and a great many trains were running, bringing up commissary supplies and taking back ordnance and other stores. At this time a great many refugees were going north on the trains. While here four hundred recruits came to us for the purpose of filling up our Regiment again, and were put in charge of Lieut. Carver until such time and opportunity came for us to re-organize, which time never came, as will appear later.

As soon as the last train had gone north the work of destroying the railroad and other property commenced. All the little towns and stations were burnt, the railroad torn up, the ties burnt and rails twisted as the army passed along. Sherman did not intend that his or any other army should ever pass that way again.

When we arrived at Atlanta we found half of it in ashes and the next day the rest of it was burnt, only a few houses escaping. On Nov. 20th Gen. Sherman set his army in motion for the memorable march to the sea.

John Wolverton, Co. E. Greensburg, Ind.

The army of the Tennessee, under Gen. O. O. Howard, and the army of Georgia Fourteenth and Twentieth corps, under command of H. W. Slocum, and a column of cavalry, under Gen. Judson Kilpatrick.

Here our small command was transferred from the supply train to corps ordnance train as guards. Our line of march was by way of Covington, Millegeville, Saundersville, Louisville, a little to the right of Waynesboro, thence down the Savannah river to the city. Just after leaving Atlanta, Lieut. Myers was authorized to borrow enough horses from the citizens to mount twenty men, whose duty it was to collect supplies for the rest of us. They were soon mounted and at work. One morning when about twenty miles below Millegeville, they were surprised by a body of Confederate cavalry, and Lieut. Myers and Private J. W. Sharp, of Co. B, and two others, were captured; two were killed, two badly wounded and left on the ground; the rest escaped.

At that time Sergeant Isaac H. Andrews, of Co. A, and two others of the same Company—old Company D, were captured, taken into the woods and shot with pistols. William Hamilton and the other one fell at the first fire. Andrews did not fall till he was shot the second time.

The rebels stood at the left and rear of their prisoners. The first ball struck Andrews at the angle of the left jaw and came out under the left eye, breaking the left jaw and cheek bone. The second shot struck behind the left ear, and coming out through the right cheek, fractured the cheek bone, knocking him down.

The rebels then took the contents of the pockets of those killed, taking one hundred and two dollars from Andrews. He could hear them talking, but could not move. One of them asked: "Have you searched all his pockets?" and was answered, "Yes." Just at that time he heard another shot and was struck in front of the right ear, the ball lodging back of his eyes, where he carried it for eight years. One day while working in the field he began to sneeze, when out dropped the ball. Sergeant Andrews says that since Nov. 25th, 1864, he has never seen a day that his head has not pained him in some way.

Elbert N. Cowan, Co. K. Monmouth, Ill.

After having lain for some time he came to, and tried to move, but was too weak. After some time he crawled over to where one of the other boys lay and found he was dead. After he had sat there for some time a negro came to him, and stooping down told him to put his arms around his neck. Then the negro carried him to a house, about a quarter of a mile, where there were two white women and some negroes. The two white women treated him kindly, dressed his wounds and made him as comfortable as possible. He was found by some of the Twenty-second Indiana boys and taken to our ambulance train that evening and hauled through to Savannah. On the 6th day of January, 1865, Sergeant Andrews being able to travel, came home on a furlough. After remaining at home thirty days, he reported at Indianapolis. As his wounds had not healed they ordered him to be taken to the hospital. He did not want to go, and was sent home for ten days longer. After this he reported again although his wounds were still running, and was given transportation to New York where he had to wait for a week. From New York he was sent to Hilton Head, S. C. He was not able to join his Regiment, and was sent up Broad river to a convalescent camp in the latter part of February, 1865. After being in this camp a few days he took erysipelas in his wounds and was sent to Beaufort, S. C., to the hospital, where he came near dying.

In March he was sent to New York to Fort Schuyler hospital, where he stayed until April, when all Indiana soldiers were ordered sent to their own State. He went to Madison, where he was discharged June 14, 1865. Comrade Andrews is still living at Osgood, Ind., at this time, May, 1896.

On Dec. 4th there was a sharp fight at Waynesboro within hearing of us. On the 10th Savannah was invested by our army and on the 12th of December Gen. Hazen's division of the Fifteenth corps captured Fort McAlister on the Oguchee river. On the 20th the Confederate army, under Gen. Hardee, evacuated the city and crossed over into South Carolina. The next day our forces took possession of it and large quantities of stores fell into our hands. The train parked near the edge of the city and we camped nearby, keeping guard over the ammunition train. There was not much fighting on the way down and we came by easy marches. Three days' rations were issued at Atlanta and a small ration at Millegeville; the rest of our supplies were taken from the country as we passed along. They consisted principally of sweet potatoes, fresh pork and molasses, which was found in ample abundance for our daily wants. But for a few days before rations could be received from the ocean transports, our supplies ran low and there was nothing in the country to get except rice and that was mostly unthrashed. The mills were set going, but were not adequate to supply the demand of the men. Yet it was a great help to tide us over the "pinch." We tried thrashing by hand and tried cooking it with the hull on, but it was "no go."

Our army moved in four columns, and a strip of country forty miles wide was cleaned of everything that was of any use to us or that could be of any use or comfort to the enemy. Our foragers gathered up all the horses, mules, cattle and everything that could be used by our army. The mules were put into the wagon trains, the horses into the batteries and the cattle were killed and the beef issued to the men. All wagons, carts, plows and implements of every description that were of any use were piled up and burned. All houses that were not occupied, barns and outhouses of every description were all burned. The men would run the grist mills until the rear guard came along, when they would be set on fire. We were not out of sight of the smoke of burning buildings from Atlanta till we got in front of Savannah.

The men with the wagon trains had to work day and night making corduroy roads and helping the wagons and batteries over the swampy places. Small streams were bridged with small trees and poles and the larger ones were pontooned.

The boys were all on the watch for something to come around looking for an owner. Some of them had a habit of looking out for themselves, and mess No. 2 was not an exception. Just before leaving Atlanta, Foster was looking around and saw a sack of coffee leaning up by itself "sort of lonesome like." His knife blade coming against it, he caught a Sibly hat full and mess No. 2 had coffee enough to last them till they got to the sea.

James Coulter, 1st Sergeant and 1st Lieutenant Co. B, Amelia, O.

On the fourth day, out from Atlanta we halted to rest in front of a house where there were chickens running around loose. A negro cook for some officers wanted some one to hold his new tin bucket while he tried to charm some of the fowls. Hollingsworth, of mess No. 2, said he would hold it, and when the cook came back with his chickens the bucket had gone off with Hollingsworth. Well, that bucket did service with No. 2 and many were the chickens and sweet potatoes that were cooked in it. At the battle of Bentonville, N. C., Hollingsworth had it on his belt when the Johnnies shot the side out of it and ruined it for further use.

Three or four days before we arrived at Savannah George Bloom and two or three others started out early in the morning foraging and went on the road on which our division was moving. There had been a rain the night before and after they had gone three or four miles, they saw a fresh wagon track in the mud. They followed it up and found a darkey, three mules and a wagon near the side of the road in a sink hole in the woods. The wagon bed was nearly full of hams and shoulders. Bloom took command; the darkey drove out to the road and waited till our wagon train came up when they fell into line with their prize. We had a good supply of hams for a few days. The darkey had been sent from our right wing to save the pork, but fell in with us. Evidently the natives did not know that we were quite so numerous and that darkey's boss lost his mules, wagon, meat, darkey and all. What

Martin Moor, Co. H.
Forest Hill, Ind.

was his loss was our gain, but we never went back to thank him for his present. Soon after getting possession of the city of Savannah our supplies were received at the wharf from the ocean vessels in great abundance. The enterprising Yankee also was there with trading vessels from the North laden with fruits, vegetables, etc., to sell to the army. Apples and oranges sold as high as fifty dollars per barrel, potatoes and onions as high as twenty dollars per barrel and fifty per cent. higher retail. Then the provost marshal interfered and prices became more reasonable.

While the Companies were near Savannah they were sent out one evening to support a battery near the fort that Gen. Lincoln had built near the old Ebenezer church that he used as a hospital in the War of the Revolution. The battery was to intercept a rebel gun boat that was reported to be up the river; but the boat failed to come, and we did not get to immortalize ourselves by blowing it out of the river or sinking it. However, some of the boys went to the cemetery and slept by the graves of the Revolutionary patriots.

On the march from Atlanta negroes of all ages, sexes, shades and grades, by the thousands followed our army, carrying a few household goods in all imaginable shapes, sizes and varieties. How they managed to subsist has always been a mystery to us. When we arrived at Savannah the able-bodied men were set to work building fortifications and the rest were sent to Hilton Head. Those four hundred recruits with which we had expected to re-organize our Regiment were taken away from us just before our arrival at Savannah and put into other Regiments; then we were doomed to remain a residuary command for the rest of our service.

About this time Lieut. Henry resigned and went home. When he reached Indianapolis he recommended to Gov. Morton that First Sergeant Thomas Kirk be commissioned First Lieutenant of Co. A—Lieut. George Myers having been captured, and that Second Lieutenant Socrates Carver, Sergeants James Coulter and Mitchell H. Day be commissioned Captain, First Lieutenant and Second Lieutenant, respectively, of Co. B. The commissions were issued to date from Dec. 24th, 1864, a Christmas gift from the Governor. The army remained at the city several weeks.

The weather was fine and we had a good time generally. While the army was at Chattanooga there was a detail made from the Regiment for guard for the first Division Quartermaster Department, and when the non-veterans returned home their places were filled from the men that remained. In all of the campaign to the sea they did their full share in all the duties that fell to their lot. They brought in a great many horses and mules and turned them over to the Quartermaster. They made a good many narrow escapes from being captured and acquired considerable skill in foraging. Some of the soldiers thought they must keep it up to a certain extent for fear they might get out of practice; so three or four of them went over to the Company one evening while they lay near Savannah, and getting some help from the Company, made a raid on a lot of provisions that some parties had stored in the back yard at a house near the Company's camp. Lieut. Carver and some of the other officers occupied the house and at the rear of the yard was a fence about eight feet high, boarded up and down. Two or three of the men were helped over and they lifted the barrels of potatoes, onions and other eatables upon the fence, where they were caught by the boys on the other side. All were carried away some distance, the barrels were emptied and the supplies divided. Our boys borrowed a mule from one of the teamsters without his consent and carried their part to their camp. The next morning there were some fellows out on the hunt for their stores. They found some empty barrels, but not the contents. However, some of the men feasted on potatoes and other vegetables for several days.

The Quartermaster kept a very good cow and his cook was very proud of her. He fed her all the forage she would eat and led her out every day to graze. With all this good care the darkey could not understand why she failed in her milk in the mornings. The soldiers had to guard her, too, with their other duties, and some of them could milk. They thought as there were several of them they would help the cook with his milking, but they always did their part early in the morning before the cook waked up. The Captain did not have so much milk for his whisky punch, but the boys had plenty for their coffee. Sergeant Tip Davis, of Co. B, was detailed as Division Ordnance Sergeant. His quarters were near the arsenal in a little frame building that was put up for the guards before we came in possession. Tip got very sick while we were in this camp and T. G. Van Meter, of Co. B, went over to be company for him one night. The next morning some of the doctors went to see Tip and said he had a very bad case of varioloid; he was then moved to the small-pox hospital. Van Meter was very much worried about his chances of becoming affected and asked his mess to not put too much seasoning in their cooking, as he wanted to diet so he would not be sick when his time came. That suited the rest of the boys first rate, as they did not have any more than they

J. S. McCullough, Co. K, Indianapolis, Ind. One of the boys who did not enlist for fun, believing the struggle would be long and bloody, but having an unwavering faith in the ultimate triumph of the right; served as private Co. K until February, '63, and balance of time on detached duty at headquarters Pioneer Brigade Army of the Cumberland.

could eat anyhow; so they put in all the seasoning they wanted and Van Meter half starved for nine days. Tom got up the ninth morning with some of Job's afflictions, and did not sit down for some days. The varioloid did not trouble him any more after that.

Savannah is a quaint looking old town, with broad but unpaved streets, and some fine monuments. About the 20th of January, 1865, our wing of the army moved out a few miles from the city and camped for a day or two, some troops from the Eastern army having arrived to garrison the city. We moved to Sister's Ferry on the Savannah river, about fifty miles above the city, and camped again. There had been heavy rains, the river was high and the lowlands on the opposite side were inundated. Here the army remained several days, partly on account of the high water and probably to get a better supply of provisions before severing connection with our base of supplies.

B. F. Denahm, Co. B. Sardinia, Ind.

In a few days the boats came up, bringing provisions, mail, etc. The wagons were loaded, the boats returned, a pontoon was laid and the army crossed over into South Carolina.

While at Sister's Ferry our three Companies, very much against our will and protest, were separated. Co. A was assigned to duty with the Thirty-eighth Indiana, Co. B to the Twenty-second Indiana and the other men were sent to the Eighty-eighth Indiana. Companies A and B were allowed to retain their Company organization, but the other men were distributed to different Companies of the Eighty-eighth Indiana. Our Co. B was now in Third Brigade, Second Division, Fourteenth A. C.; Co. A and the other men were in the First Division Fourteenth A. C. Our Brigade was composed of Twenty-second Indiana, Fifty-second Ohio, Eighty-fifth, Eighty-sixth and One Hundred and Twenty-fifth Illinois, and was commanded by Brevet Brigadier Gen. Fearing. Capt. William Snodgrass was in command of the Twenty-second Indiana. He was a rough man, but kind to his men and brave to a fault. This was one of the oldest Regiments in the service, first commanded by Jeff. C. Davis, who was at this time commanding the Fourteenth Corps. The boys of the Twenty-second were a brave, generous-hearted set of fellows and we became very much attached to them.

Our line of march was by way of Lawtonville, Barnwell Court House, Columbia and Winsboro, S. C., and from Fayetteville to Goldsboro, N. C. It was early in February when the army set out to go through the Carolinas. The recent heavy rains had swollen the streams and filled the Edisto Swamp. At times it was difficult to make headway, sometimes having to wade for hours through water knee deep and deeper, always cold and frequently icy. When near Columbia the right wing of the army joined ours from the East. At Columbia the enemy showed a disposition to fight. We were formed into a line of battle, but before we got in sight of town the Johnnies fled. John Coiles, of Co. A. was killed here.

Our wing of the army passed to the left of Columbia, crossed the Saluda and Broad rivers, then stopped a day or two to destroy a railroad. Our Regiment (the Twenty-second Indiana), was the first to cross Broad river, going over in pontoon boats and standing guard while the bridge was being put down. While crossing the Wateree river a heavy rain came, and the river rising suddenly, the bridge gave way. It was several days before all got over and under headway again. Here service was required that tried the patience and endurance of the men; working in the rain and mud day and night getting the teams over the rivers and hills—a pension hater's "picnic." One evening we were detailed to assist the wagon trains over the worst roads that we ever saw. It was a partly decayed corduroy or plank road and we had about six minutes to make camp. There would be a few rods of reasonably good road, then there would be a hole without any bottom, apparently; the mules would be unable to extricate the wagons, and then we would have to put our shoulders to the wheels. By dint of much loving talk to the mules by the teamsters and much lifting on our part, with a few cheering words from the wagon masters, we would finally get the wagons out of the hole only to have to help the next one. We covered the six miles by about eight o'clock the next morning, a muddy, tired and wet lot of men. This night's work was through a turpentine forest in which the trees had been scored for a number of feet from the ground. After dark the exuded sap was fired on the trees for quite a distance from the road. Taking the swearing by the teamsters and the wagon masters, the struggling mules, the jerking and rumbling of the wagons on the planks and the jokes or ejaculations of the men with the fantastic shadows cast by the struggling men, mules and wagons, made a sight worthy of a painter.

After this we came into a better country. There was a Confederate force a few miles below us on the Great Pedee river—the right wing having run them away and they were supposed to be in our front on the opposite side of the river. Here occurred one of those incidents that helped to make soldiering interesting as well as somewhat perilous. Our Co. B was stationed at the ferry to watch and report if there were any of the enemy about. All being quiet, the pontooners came at midnight, put a few boats together, launched them, and our Company getting in, pulled across. It was very dark and we drifted some distance, but finally reached the other shore and scrambled up the bank as fast as we could. We found ourselves in a dense thicket of underbrush, but fortunately no enemy. Then the Regiment followed in like manner, and a little after daylight the bridge was completed, when troops, trains and all passed over in safety. But we felt a little "shaky" at first, as we did not know what kind of a reception awaited us over there.

W. A. Wayland, Private Co. A. born in 1845; mustered in July 25, 1861; mustered out Aug. 1, 1865. Beulah, Col.

The next place of interest in our course was Fayetteville, N. C. This was a small town of ancient appearance, situated on the south side of Cape Fear river. It was said to have been of considerable importance to the confederacy, as great quantities of ordnance were made there during the war. March 12th, 1865, our "bummers" drove away a small force and captured the place before the head of the column came up. George Bloom and one or two others of our Company were in the engagement. The army rested here two or three days.

On March 16th our cavalry got into an engagement with the enemy about twenty miles north of Fayetteville, at Aversboro, and were getting the worst of it when the infantry came up to assist them. Our Brigade was on the extreme left of the line reaching to Cape Fear river, and was the last to get in. It was about night when we got in front of the enemy's works and the fight was nearly over. However, the Regiment lost several men, killed and wounded. Ed McCullum, of our Company, was wounded Some of the boys regretted that they lost all their rations. Mess No. 2 lost their sack of sweet potatoes and had no supper. Next morning Andy Bell came up with a few peas and they had peas for breakfast. Our cavalry lost a good many men; they also killed and captured a good many of the enemy, among others the notorious Gen. Rhette, of South Carolina. The enemy retreated during the night, and on the morning of the 17th our forces moved forward again, meeting no serious opposition until the 19th when near Bentonville, N. C. Here were the combined forces of Gen. Joe Johnson and others entrenched across our road. The First and Second Division Fourteenth A. C. were in advance and came rather unexpectedly on the Confederates, who came out of their works. After some severe fighting our lines fell back some distance, when the Twentieth corps came up and the Johnnies were driven back to their works with heavy loss, leaving many of their dead

Milton G. Moor, Co. H.
Forest Hill, Ind.

and wounded in our hands. Granville Smith, a young recruit of Co. B, captured a Confederate picket the next morning as he was sitting asleep by a tree, and turned him over to the Brigade Commander. Granville was very proud of his prize.

Our forces followed up within a short distance of the enemy's works, and entrenching themselves waited for the other wing of our army to come to our assistance. On the afternoon of the 21st they struck the Confederate left and in a short time the whole rebel army was flying across the country. The battle of Bentonville was comparatively a small affair, yet it was a very severe one considering the number of troops engaged. The loss on our side was considerable, and the Confederate loss was supposed to be greater. The Twenty-second Indiana lost thirty-four men, killed and wounded, our Company losing three in wounded. Gen. Fearing, Brigade Commander, was severely wounded in the hand. Lieutenant-Colonel Langley, of the One Hundred and Twenty-fifth Illinois, assumed command of the Brigade and retained it till the close of the war. Edward Schofield, originally of Co. B, but serving with Co. I Eighty-eighth Indiana, was killed. The writer has not been able to learn what part was taken by the rest of the Thirty-seventh.

On the morning of March 22d, the road being clear, our army set out for Goldsboro, twenty miles distant, and reached that point on the 24th. March 10th Isaac Wilkinson, Levi Cochran and Samuel Taten were captured while out foraging. Wilkinson said the first thing his captors asked for was his money and watch. In their hurry they did not take time to search him, so he gave them a small amount of change he had in one pocket, and while hurrying him out through the swamp for fear they might be captured themselves, he threw away his pocketbook and watch. He thinks if he were down there now he could find it. After they got their prisoners away some distance from the road they commenced to trade hat and boots with them. They traded hat and boots three times with Wilkinson, and when the fourth one wanted to trade Ike told him to keep the whole outfit. He thinks he did the poorest trading he ever did in his life. After they were taken inside of the enemy's lines their horses were taken from them and they marched two days and nights bare-footed and bare-headed. At Goldsboro a junction was formed with the Fourth and Twenty-third corps under Gen. Schofield, the Tenth corps under Gen. Terry and all under command of Gen. Sherman. We now felt superior to the combined forces of the Confederacy.

Here ended the Carolina campaign. It had been the hardest campaign we had ever experienced, not in fighting, but in marching and exposure. For two months in the winter season we had been on the march, had passed entirely through one State and a part of two others, waded creeks and swamps and mud. We had slept on the damp ground with little shelter from the elements, and often with but scant rations. Hundreds of men were hatless and shoeless, and all as black as Africans from standing around pine knot fires. It was very trying on the health and endurance of the men, yet no one murmured. It had rained fifteen days and nights since we crossed the Savannah river at Sister's Ferry, and the roads were in a very bad condition, almost impassable in many places—not a very desirable place for "picknicking."

The country through which we passed was generally very poor, there being much pine forest and many turpentine camps. The latter made fine bonfires. Very little property of any kind escaped destruction in South Carolina, but in North Carolina dwellings were generally spared. Almost everything else was taken or destroyed. Goldsboro was a dilapidated town near the Neuse river, and in a fairly good farming country.

April 10th, 1865. This morning our army is again on the march, now in the direction of Raleigh, which place was reached on the 13th. It was a small, quaint, old town, surrounded by a jungle of underbrush and the poorest excuse for a State capital we ever saw. When nearing Raleigh, mess No. 2 thought they would put on a little style, so they got them a negro to cook and carry the cooking utensils. In the morning after reaching the city, the negro, having had the cramp the night before, died while they were eating breakfast.

On the 15th our corps, being in the advance, reached Haywood, a small town on the Cape Fear river, and about thirty miles southwest of Raleigh. On the 12th we received the news of the surrender of Lee's army. Our troops were wild with excitement and made the woods ring with their cheering. On the 15th three of our Company—Mike Grob, Myer Bowers and Fred Aman were taken prisoners while foraging and taken to Johnson's camp; but in a few days they were released and returned to us near Raleigh. There was no fighting after leaving Goldsboro except a little skirmishing. The last man we saw who was killed in battle was a captain in some Ohio Regiment who was killed April 10th while on the skirmish line, and some of his men

J. H. Wooley, Co. E.
Arkansas City, Kas.

were in the act of hurrying him by the roadside as we passed by. Our portion of the army remained at the Cape Fear river while negotiations for the surrender of Johnson's army were pending. Upon the capitulation of Johnson's army we were officially informed that the war was over. This caused not only great rejoicing in our army, but it was also glad tidings to the hundreds of Johnnies whom we saw returning to their homes. But many a poor, misguided fellow found, upon returning, only a chimney and a pile of ashes to mark the place he once called home. At about the same time we received the news of the assassinatian of President Lincoln, which cast a gloom of sorrow over the army.

On April 21st we moved back to near a place called Holly Springs, some fifteen miles west of Raleigh. This was considered our first day's march toward home. One night there was very heavy musket firing out two or three miles toward the front, and some staff officers went out pell mell to learn the cause. They returned shortly and reported it to be a Brigade out there jollifying. Of course the officers did not enjoy getting out at midnight, and strict orders were issued against firing after that. Our camp was pleasantly situated in the woods, and the weather was delightful. There was some very good farming land here and the crops were promising; the wheat was knee high and the

William Miles, Co. G.
Whitcomb, Ind.

corn large enough to work. The surplus stock, mules, etc., belonging to our army were turned over to the citizens to assist them in growing their crops. About a week after coming to Holly Springs we were ordered to prepare to march to Richmond, Va., and this was the first time in nearly four years of army service that we were informed of our destination before getting there.

May 1st the four corps that marched with Sherman to the sea set out for Richmond, each on a different road, and each ambitious to be the first to get through. Our corps carried off that honor, the distance being about one hundred and fifty or sixty miles, and was marched in seven days. The men were in light marching order, carrying only a few rounds of ammunition and a small quantity of provisions. The weather was warm and we marched very fast. Many men fell out by the way exhausted, and some died from over-marching. Orders were strict against foraging and destroying property, yet we did now and then take the top rail off the fence to make a fire with which to prepare our meals. We camped on the south of James river, near Richmond, and the sutlers that came out to make their "stake" off of Sherman's army were disappointed, for we had not received any pay for several months. However, we did not propose to be aggravated by having good things around and not have some of them. In the evening there could be seen a good many sutler tents, but the next morning they had all gone and their goods were distributed pretty well through Sherman's army.

Our army was to have been reviewed here at Richmond by Gen. Halleck, but Gen. Sherman came up just then—having come around from North Carolina by water, and objected. The order was countermanded and we were glad of it, as reviews were never desirable. Thanks to Gen. Sherman, we thought we had done enough of that kind of service. The most notable object we noticed in Richmond was Libby prison, where so many of our men were confined during the war. Richmond, like most southern towns, was a back number—behind the times in point of modern improvements. In the State house park was a fine equestrian statue of Washington, surrounded by a group of statues of old Virginia statesmen—fine pieces of art, but they must have looked a little out of place in the Confederate capitol.

On the 11th of May the march was resumed, this time for Washington City. Just after we had passed through Richmond we were halted, probably to let the citizens dispose of their garden vegetables, cakes and such things as they supposed the soldiers had been having a surfeit of for some time. We remember one Confederate had a pudding baked in a pan something smaller than a dish pan; somehow it disappeared and there was the most astonished look on that man's face that we ever saw. After the officers supposed we had time to buy the supplies, we were ordered to fall in, and resumed our march. The citizens had disposed of their truck, the boys had eaten it and we suppose have not yet returned to pay for it. We marched by way of Hanover Court House, Kelly's Ford, Bull Run battle-field and Fairfax Court House, and camped May 18th on the height between Washington and Alexandria, and in sight of the National capital. Here we remained until after the grand review.

All Companies had their odd characters, and Co. B was no exception. After leaving Richmond one of our Company was missing, and on our march to Washington there was some talk among the boys as to what should be done with him for playing off on this march. Capt. Carver promised to punish him for it. The next morning, after we arrived near the city, Bowers came up and the Captain took him to task for not marching through with the Company. Bowers said he had marched as much in this "tam war" as he intended to, so he took passage by water and came around. The Captain took a rope and tied Bowers' hands behind his back, then tied him to a small tree. After some time the officers' cook got their breakfast ready and they sat down to eat. Presently Bowers remarked to the Captain that it looked hard for him to be tied after he had marched nearly all over the Confederacy, and to stand there without any breakfast while the rest were eating and enjoying themselves. The Captain asked him if he had not had his breakfast, then got up, untied him and told him to sit down and eat with them. Bowers told the Captain all about his trip and of all the sights he had seen in Washington and how he had enjoyed himself. The officer was much interested and when breakfast was over allowed Bowers to remain released. We were on grand review May 24th, then went into camp about two miles north of the city in a beautiful grove near the Soldiers' Home. Congress was not in session and we had the privilege of going through the Capitol and other public places at will. We were not slow to improve our opportunities. The country between Richmond and Washington looked very desolate, having been occupied and over-run for years by contending

John Patton, First Sergeant Co. K; died of wounds Feb. 13, 1863, received at Stone river Dec. 31, 1862.

armies. There were no inhabitants, no buildings, no stock, no crops and the land was a poor, dreary waste. The only good country we remember to have seen in the State was the Roanoke Valley. It appeared to have been in a high state of cultivation previous to the war. Hanover Court House was a very plain looking building, constructed in colonial times and made of brick imported from England. Fairfax was a small, obsolete looking place, and is frequently mentioned in the histories of the war. When we reached Washington City, our active soldier life was at an end; the last battle had been fought, the last march had been made, the flag had been restored and peace reigned supreme. Troops were being mustered out every day, but the western troops of Sherman's army were sent to Louisville, Ky., to be mustered out.

Levi Nutt, Co. B.
Summitsville, Ind.

The last year's campaign had been very arduous and enervating, to say nothing about the many hard-fought battles, thrilling adventures and hair-breadth escapes. The men as a rule appeared to stand the hardships very well at the time, but when peace came their systems gave way to the great physical strain they were so long under, and a large per cent. of them became unfit for further service. Many succumbed and few entirely recovered. Just before leaving Washington, Co. B was detailed as guards at headquarters second division Fourteenth A. C., under Gen. James D. Morgan. On the 13th of June we left the city via Baltimore & Ohio railroad, took the steamer Lady Grace at Parkersburg, and arrived at Louisville on the 18th. We went into camp a mile east of the city, near the work-house pike, and this was our last camping place. While here we were camped near a dairy and the boys used to go over of nights and milk the cows. The dairyman objected to our help and went to headquarters and asked to have a guard detailed to watch his cows. Fred Aman was detailed as guard, but all the arrest he made was a coffee-pot, the boys giving him the slip and getting away.

As guards at headquarters, our duties were light; we were not under much restraint and had a good time generally. A good many of the boys went home on French leave, but returned in due time. July 24th, 1865, mustered rolls were signed and final papers were prepared. A few days later all of the two Companies went up to Indianapolis, the detachment having been mustered out with the Thirty-eighth Indiana on the 15th of July. Gov. Morton and other State officers met us with a kindly greeting. We stayed in the city two or three days and Aug. 1st received final pay and discharges from Uncle Sam's army. Then we scattered to our several homes, few of us ever to meet again. Of the one hundred stalwart young patriots that composed our Company (B), at Lawrenceburg four years before, only twenty-five were present at the final muster out of the Company at the close of the war. Some had been killed in battle, some died of wounds, others of disease, and some had been discharged on account of wounds and other disabilities. But all had discharged their obligations to the best of their abilities and opportunities. "Peace hath her victories not less renowned than war."

To the friends and living comrades of the Thirty-seventh Residuary Battalion Indiana Veteran Volunteer Infantry, and to the memory of those who have answered the last roll call this history is respectfully inscribed. After thirty years have passed, it is not easy to write a history of the thrilling experiences and exciting scenes of our service, with but little reliable data and very deficient memories from which to draw. It has been our constant aim to be correct and to obtain as reliable data as possible.

We wish to acknowledge our obligations to Comrades James Coulter, Mitchel H. Day, Tip Davis, Isaac H. Andrews, John F. Wolverton, Edwin E. Druley, Ellis W. Foster, Levi L. Bond, James S. Greenlee, Thomas G. Van Meter and Isaac Wilkinson for their assistance and kind words of encouragement to us, in the work of compiling the matter herein contained.

May this short history recall many recollections of our service and bring about the renewal of comradeships almost forgotten. May the coming years crown each comrade with plenty, peace and honor, as full and free as his loyal service in defense of the Union deserves, is the wish of their comrade. JAMES W. SCOTT.

[The following was written by Comrade Alexander S. Butler:]

After the Thirty-seventh left for home, their time of service having about expired, Gen. Hood began a movement to Gen. Sherman's rear, intending, no doubt, to cut off supplies and capture all army stores in his rear. The events that occurred at Allatoona furnished the facts for the song, "Hold the Fort." By so doing he would be compelled to retreat out of, not only Atlanta, but out of Georgia and Tennessee as well. The movement in that direction was followed up for a time. When the object was understood, Gen. Sherman stopped the pursuit and returned to Atlanta. Co. B being in the movement, and only got as far north as Ackworth. The Company guarded forage there a day or two, the only duty so far. While the writer of this was on duty at about 9 o'clock p. m., a line officer approached to say that a sack of corn had been stolen and was abandoned for fear of capture. A Corporal was called and sent for it. It proved to be coffee; had been stolen from cars near by. Could a soldier steal something to eat from his government?

The above incidents occurred about the first and second weeks in October, 1864. We remained at Atlanta about a month. The movement to the sea was begun on the 14th of November. Co. B being in the city, was about the last to leave. We saw several warehouses of cotton consumed. We commenced our tramp with the artillery corps. It was march, and no duty; monotonous for a month. A very few places are remembered. Covington and Millegeville, the capital of Georgia, are remembered. At the latter place a few men wearing striped clothing were seen.

L. L. Bond, Co. B. Quakertown, Ind.

The weather was dry and pleasant and the roads good. When we got to the Savannah river we crossed a broad swamp on a graded road, with a trestle bridge that had an outlet a little way to the left through a deep cut just at the river. Co. B was located in it just at night, to intercept a rebel gunboat that had just gone up the river. We were there all night, but saw no boat. A day or two before we arrived at the swamp the corps Quartermaster passed the writer as he tramped alone, saluted and said he would like some of that coffee at Ackworth. An explanation was asked and one given, and so passed on.

That night we had some coffee and crackers issued to us—the first on the trip. It showed, too, that rations could be had without a requisition. At Savannah we got nothing but coffee and rice at the first. While at Savannah we went where and when we pleased, and stayed as long. When we went to the Savannah river at the landing, eighteen miles from the ocean, we marched down the streets or near the buildings and went over or around the stoops (porticos), they extending into or across the sidewalk, and some of them two or three feet high.

To go back to the "swamp." There was a brick church there, built in 1765. The bricks were imported from England. Unpainted, hard, pine seats and elevated pulpit, with columns supporting the roof, made it look old. I wondered, while up in the pulpit looking down at the boys, who had strolled into it, if the Johnnies had taught the 13th chapter of Romans, or if their preachers had. It has taken a good deal of writing to tell about watching for that gunboat that night. In doing so I have told Co. B's history as it was worked out. The Company made one foraging trip and got but little or nothing.

When we were ordered to, we started North with the rest of the boys. In two or three days we got up to Sister's Ferry, where we crossed over to South Carolina (ancient secessions); were detained there a little. During the time Co. B did something else. Gen. Jefferson C. Davis had ordered Co. B to report to the Twenty-second Indiana Infantry two or three different times. We had all agreed to not do it. At the ferry Gen. Davis sent an orderly with a request, verbal, I believe for the Captain and a Sergeant to come to his tent. It was to ask why Co. B did not obey his orders to report to the Twenty-second Infantry. The Captain told the General that we had not refused to do duty, that we would do any duty ordered, but that we would not consent to a disbanding of the Company; so we went with the Twenty-second Indiana and retained our organization until mustered out of the service. That was the status of the Company when the writer and all the members of the Company whose term expired before Oct. 1st, 1865. I do not know now whether that order applied to the drafted men or not. The Company was organized under an order from a ranking officer. Gen. Jeff. C. Davis could not compel us to go, nor could he disband the Company. Co. A was disbanded at the time the Regiment left for Indianapolis, I think. I know nothing at all of it or of the detachment. They were in a different part of the army—probably with Gen. Thomas' army at Nashville.

The whole march to Savannah and also from Savannah to Raleigh, N. C., was uneventful. We crossed several streams on pontoon bridges; had little to do; only a little at Bentonville; lived on yams mostly; got a little fresh pork at times; had crackers and coffee all the time, and have no recollection of doing guard or picket duty on the whole march around to Washington. We went along with the boys after the battle of Bentonville and the surrender of Johnson's army in the vicinity of Raleigh, N. C. Sherman's army made a race for Washington. Home with a discharge seemed near and gave spring to the muscles and satisfaction to the mind. The writer did not march, but went to New Berne by rail and up the Albemarle and Pamlico sounds and Elizabeth river to Norfolk, and across the Hampton roads to Fortress Monroe; then up Chesapeake Bay and Potomac river to Alexandria, where the troops were encamped. Then came the review. I send a clipping from a newspaper, from Gen. Grant's memoirs. It gives a better idea of the review than I can write:

"On the 18th of May orders were issued by the Adjutant-General for a grand review, by the President and his Cabinet, of Sherman's and Meade's armies. The review commenced on the 22d, and lasted two days. Meade's army occupied over six hours of the first day in passing the grand stand, which had been erected in front of the President's house. Sherman witnessed this review from the grand stand, which was occupied by the President and his Cabinet. * * * Sherman's troops had been in camp on the south side of the Potomac. During the night of the 23d he crossed over and bivouacked not far from the Capitol. Promptly at 10 o'clock on the morning of the 24th his troops commenced to pass in review. Sherman's army made a different appearance from that of the army of the Potomac. The latter had been operating where they received directly from the North full supplies of food and clothing regularly. The review of this army therefore was the review of a body of 65,000 well-drilled, well-disciplined and orderly soldiers, inured to hardship and fit for any duty, but without the experience of gathering their own food and supplies in an enemy's country, and of being ever on the watch. Sherman's army was not so well dressed as the army of the Potomac, but their marching could not be excelled; they gave the appearance of men who had been thoroughly drilled to endure hardships, either by long and continuous marches or through exposure to any climate, without the ordinary shelter of a camp. They exhibited also some of the order of march through Georgia where the "sweet potatoes sprung up from the ground," as Sherman's army went marching through. In the rear of a Company there would be a captured horse or mule loaded with small cooking utensils, captured chickens and other food picked up for the use of the men. Negro families who had followed the army would sometimes come along in the rear of the Company, with three or four children packed upon a single mule, and the mother leading it.

"The sight was varied and grand. Nearly all day for two successive days, from the Capitol to the Treasury Building, could be seen a mass of orderly soldiers marching in columns of Companies. The National flag was flying from almost every house and store; the windows were filled with spectators; the doorsteps and sidewalks were crowded with colored people and poor whites who did not succeed in securing better quarters from which to get a view of the grand armies. The city was about as full of strangers who had come to see the sights as it usually is on inauguration day, when a new President takes his seat."

After this we had a free visit to all the public buildings of the Capitol, as well as the Capitol itself. The muster out and the sluggish trip home. A little delayed by red tape at Indianapolis and we were soon at home on June 18th, 1865.   A. S. BUTLER.

Residuary Battalion Co. A.

Captain—
 Myers, George, not mustered as Captain; prisoner of war, captured Nov. 25, '64.

First Lieutenant—
 Kirk, Thomas, mustered out with battalion.

First Sergeant—
 Nelson, Devastus W., mustered out July 25, '65.

Sergeants—
 Cravens, Wesley, mustered out July 25, '65.
 Castetter, Ira, mustered out July 25, '65.
 Andrews, Isaac H., mustered out June 14, '65.
 Starkey, Thomas, mustered out June 14, '65.

Corporals—
 Stephens, Benjamin, mustered out July 25, '65.
 Kennedy, John E., mustered out July 25, '65.
 Uppinghouse, Eli F., mustered out July 25, '65.
 Meek, James H., mustered out July 25, '65.
 Grecian, Isaac, mustered out July 25, '65.
 Myers, James C., mustered out July 25, '65, as Sergeant.
 Backert, Joseph, mustered out as Sergeant.
 Burlban, John, transferred to V. R. C. March 22, '65.

Privates—
 Buchannan, John, mustered out July 25, '65.
 Brown, Harrison, mustered out July 25, '65.
 Brown, James P., mustered out July 25, '65.
 Bodine, Jeremiah M., mustered out July 25, '65.
 Bohlander, John, mustered out July 25, '65.
 Coplinger, Jacob M., mustered out July 25, '65.
 Cole, William, mustered out July 25, 65.
 Curren, Newton, mustered out July 25, '65.
 Crane, Cornelius E., mustered out July 25, '65.
 Corlin, Philip, mustered out July 25, '65.
 Carpenter, Oliver, mustered out July 25, '65.

Cox, William A., mustered out July 25, '65.
Cameron, John, mustered out July 25, '65.
Christopher, Michael, mustered out July 25, '65.
Cooney, John, killed at Broad River, S. C., Feb. 19, '65.
Coiles, John, killed at Columbia, S. C., Feb. 19, '65.
Cochran, Levi, mustered out June 17, '65.
Day, Mahlon, mustered out July 25, '65.
Davis, Guilford D., mustered out July 25, '65.
Dickerson, Newton, mustered out July 25, '65.
Dunn, Samuel H., mustered out July 25, '65.
Dalrymple, Charles, mustered out July 25, '65.
Edens, Ezekiel, mustered out July 25, '65.
Francisco, Obadiah A., mustered out July 25, '65, as Corporal.
French, Thomas, mustered out July 25, '65.
Grey, Thomas, mustered out July 25, '65.
Gibson, Charles, mustered out July 25, '65.
Geokins, Harrison, died at Savannah, Ga., Jan. 19, '65.
Horning, Lewis, mustered out July 25, '65.
Horning, Andrew, mustered out July 25, '65.
Hamilton, William, killed at Lewisville, Ga., Nov. 25, '64.
Hallet, John, mustered out July 25, '65.
Hanna, John, mustered out July 25, '65.
Heller, John, mustered out July 25, '65.
Hess, Theodore, mustered out July 25, '65.
Hollensbee, Edward, mustered out July 25, '65.
Hoffmaster, Frederick, mustered out July 25, '65.
Hanna, David, mustered out July 25, '65.
Harry, James, mustered out July 25, '65.
Jones, Stephen, mustered out July 25, '65.
Kelley, William R., mustered out July 25, '65.
Kinney, John, mustered out July 25, '65.
Killy, Barnard, mustered out July 25, '65.
Love, Lewis, mustered out July 25, '65.
Love, George W., mustered out July 25, '65.

Langly, Peter, mustered out July 25, '65.
Linville, Thomas, mustered out July 25, '65.
Live, Harrison, mustered out June 17, '65.
Morgan, Warren, mustered out June 17, '65.
Maynard, Henry, discharged March 14, '65, for disability.
McNew, John J., mustered out July 25, '65.
Newberry, Granville, mustered out July 25, '65.
Payton, John C., mustered out July 25, '65.
Powell, John, mustered out July 25, '65.
Purnell, Robert L., mustered out July 25, '65.
Payne, William H., mustered out July 25, '65.
Owen, John J., mustered out July 25, '65.
Sutton, Reuben, mustered out July 25, '65.
Swing, Jeremiah, mustered out July 25, '65.
Stark, Thomas, mustered out July 25, '65.
Stark, Benjamin F., mustered out July 25, '65.
Sage, Elihu, mustered out July 25, '65.
Snyder, John, mustered out July 25, '65.
Spears, John, mustered out July 25, '65.
Stoll, John G., mustered out July 25, '65.
Spears, Joseph J., mustered out June 17, '65.
Sanders, George W., mustered out June 17, '65.
Summerville, James W., mustered out July 25, '65.
Ward, Jonathan B., mustered out Dec. 16, '64.
Wayland, William A., mustered out July 25, '65.
Wright, George W., mustered out July 25, '65.
Wright, James, mustered out July 25, '65.
Widener, Leonard, mustered out July 25, '65.
Widener, Abram T., mustered out July 25, '65.
Williamson, John, mustered out July 25, '65.

Recruits—
Buckmaster, Cyrus, mustered out July 25, '65.
Dunlap, Samuel, mustered out July 25, '65.
Fox, John, mustered out July 25, '65.

Gookins, Harrison, died at Savannah, Ga., Jan. 19, '65.
Graul, Joseph, mustered out July 25, '65.
Hablizel, John, mustered out July 25, '65.
Hampton, Hiram L., mustered out July 25, '65.
Holbrook, Lucien P., mustered out July 25, '65.
Hilton, Elbridge G., mustered out July 25, '65.
Jerraid, William, mustered out July 25, '65.
Dayton, Joseph W., mustered out June 15, '65.
Proctor, Thomas, mustered out July 25, '65.
Reeder, Samuel, mustered out July 25, '65.
Shinabarger, Hugh P., mustered out July 25, '65.
Shinabarger, John H., mustered out June 21, '65.
Shinabarger, John, mustered out June 21, '65.
Whitcomb, Orletus P., mustered out June 21, '65.

Residuary Battalion Co. B.

Captain—
  Carver, Socrates, mustered out with battalion.
First Lieutenant—
  Coulter, James, mustered out with battalion.
Second Lieutenant—
  Day, Mitchel H., mustered out with battalion.
First Sergeant—
  Davis, Marion, mustered out July 25, '65.
Sergeants—
  Barnard, James C., mustered out July 25, '65.
  Foster, Ellis W., mustered out July 25, '65.
  Hollingsworth, Joseph, mustered out July 25, '65.
  Childs, Edwin R., mustered out July 25, '65.
Corporals—
  Nutt, Levi, mustered out July 25, '65.
  Bell, Andrew M., mustered out July 25, '65.
  McCullum, Edward, mustered out July 25, '65.
  Winans, William F., mustered out July 25, '65.
  Winans, Frazier N., mustered out July 25, '65.
  Force, Nelson K., mustered out July 25, '65.

Vogan, George W., mustered out July 25, '65.
Bartlow, James H., mustered out July 25, '65.

Privates—
Anderson, Lucius L., mustered out July 25, '65.
Aman, Frederick, mustered out July 25, '65.
Butler, Alexander S., mustered out June 9, '65.
Brown, Theodore T., mustered out July 25, '65.
Burgess, Joseph G., mustered out July 25, '65.
Baker, Stephen, mustered out July 25, '65.
Baker, Joshua, mustered out July 25, '65.
Barnard, Oliver W., mustered out July 25, '65.
Bloom, George, mustered out July 25, '65.
Bowers, Myer, mustered out July 25, '65.
Bowen, Thomas J., mustered out July 25, '65.
Bastian, Sibrant, mustered out July 25, '65.
Bainbridge, George W., mustered out July 25, '65.
Bond, Levi L., mustered out July 25, '65.
Daniels, William S., mustered out July 25, '65.
Davis, Charles L., mustered out July 25, '65.
Davis, Allen, mustered out July 25, '65.
Emmett, William, mustered out July 25, '65.
Edwards, Robert H., died at Chattanooga June 7, '64.
Forrer, Martin H., mustered out July 25, '65.
Graper, William F., died at Chattanooga Aug. 20, '64.
Goltry, David, mustered out July 25, '65.
Grob, Michael, mustered out July 25, '65.
Green, James A., mustered out July 25, '65.
Guire, John H., mustered out July 25, '65.
Harvey, William W., mustered out July 25, '65.
Hooks, George W., mustered out July 25, '65.
Hearn, William T., mustered out June 17, '65.
Harwood, Joseph, mustered out June 8, '65.
Johnston, William F., mustered out May 19, '65.
Kennett, Wiley, mustered out July 25, '65.
Kennett, Abram G., mustered out June 9, '65.

Kempner, William L., mustered out July 25, '65.
Long, Woodson, mustered out July 25, '65.
Lines, William M., died at Nashville Feb. 9, '65.
Mitchell, David L., mustered out June 9, '65.
Monroe, Calvin, discharged May 22, '65, disability.
Marquette, Jacob J., mustered out July 25, '65.
McClain, Robert, mustered out July 25, '65.
McClain, Tilford, mustered out July 25, '65.
Morton, John, mustered out July 25, '65.
Moore, Craven B., mustered out July 25, '65.
Miller, William H., mustered out July 25, '65.
Mitchell, Daniel, mustered out July 25, '65.
Mullen, James M., mustered out July 25, '56.
Phillips, William, mustered out July 25, '65.
Phillips, Eli, mustered out July 25, '65.
Roszell, Thomas, mustered out July 25, 65.
Reser, James H., mustered out July 25, '65.
Stringer, James B., discharged Nov. 23, '64, disability.
Smith, James, mustered out July 25, '65.
Sharp, James W., mustered out July 25, '65.
Scott, James W., mustered out July 25, '65.
Taten, Samuel, mustered out June 17, '65.
Thorn, John D., mustered out June 9, '65.
Thompson, Samuel, mustered out July 25, '65.
Van Meter, Thomas G., mustered out July 25, '65.
Wilkinson, Isaac, mustered out June 17, '65.
Wolstenholm, John, mustered out July 25, '65.
Whitcomb, Lyman, mustered out July 25, '65.
Yates, John, mustered out July 25, '65.

Recruits—
Brown, Henry, mustered out July 25, '65.
Criswell, James W., mustered out July 25, '65.
Druley, Edwin E., mustered out July 25, '65.
Foster, William, mustered out July 25, '65.
Green, Edward M., mustered out July 25, '65.

Greenwell, William, mustered out June 9, '65.
Hand, Robert S., mustered out July 25, '65.
Jones, James H., mustered out June 9, '65.
Jones, Thomas E., mustered out June 9, '65.
Lane, Edwin, mustered out June 9, '65.
Lichtenberger, Peter, mustered out June 29, '65.
Mitchell, Milton A., mustered out June 9, '65.
Martin, Asa.
Newman, Philip W., mustered out July 25, '65.
Nichols, Peter L., mustered out June 3, '65.
Pence, Lewis M., mustered out July 25, '65.
Robins, James, mustered out July 25, '65.
Robinson, James, mustered out July 25, '65.
Smith, Granville, mustered out July 25, '65.
Schweigert, Henry, mustered out July 25, '65.
Sefirt, William W., mustered out June 9, '65.
Stull, John, mustered out June 9, '65.
St. Clair, Jesse, mustered out June 9, '65.
Tatman, William, mustered out July 25, '65.
Thompson, John N., mustered out July 25, '65.
Waters, Hosea M., died at Rockingham, N. C., March 8, '65.
Williams, Denton, mustered out June 29, '65.
Wyland, Benjamin F., mustered out June 9, '65.
Yoder, John H., mustered out June 9, '65.
Zeitler, Wolfgang, mustered out June 9, '65.

Detachment Thirty-seventh Indiana, Commanded by Sergeant John F. Wolverton.

Beck, Frederick.
Brooks, Lewis C.
Bartlow, William H.
Clark, Benjamin F.
Cook, Abram.
Daily, Barton N.

Denham, James B.
Denham, Benjamin.
Fisher, James A.
Fox, John H.
Gamber, John.
George, Atwell.
Greenlee, James L.
Hamlin, John.
Hamlin, Omer.
Keeler, Ira M.
Keeler, John M.
Kelly, William.
Knapp, Abram.
Larue, George N.
Liming, Robert.
Lowes, Cyrenus S.
Martin, Milton.
McKeeon, William.
McKee, James C.
McNeely, Birt.
Millspaugh, George C.
Rutherford, Anderson.
Scott, Samuel.
Scott, Joseph A.
Schofield, Edward, killed at Bentonville, N. C.
Sizelove, Joseph R.
Shafer, Henry J.
Stopper, William.
True, Thomas F.
Taylor, Squire A.
Ward, James A.
Wilson, Milton M., mustered out as Sergeant.
Wooley, James H., mustered out as Sergeant.
Wood, Thomas J.
Woodard, Charles W.

www.ingramcontent.com/pod-product-compliance
Lightning Source LLC
Chambersburg PA
CBHW021812230426
43669CB00008B/725